SCOTLAND'S
MALT WHISKY DISTILLERIES

SCOTLAND'S
MALT WHISKY DISTILLERIES

JOHN HUGHES

TEMPUS

Title page: *Barnard described Ardbeg's situation on the south-east coast of Islay as 'in a lonely spot on the very edge of the sea, and its isolation tends to heighten the romantic sense of its position'.*

This page: *Two Pagodas at Glentauchers distillery.*

First published 2002
This revised edition 2003

Tempus Publishing Limited
The Mill, Brimscombe Port,
Stroud, Gloucestershire, GL5 2QG

www.tempus-publishing.com

British Library Cataloguing in Publication Data.
A catalogue record for this book is available from the British Library.

ISBN 0 7524 2592 7

Typesetting and origination by Tempus Publishing Limited
Printed in Great Britain by Midway Colour Print, Wiltshire

This book is dedicated to my wife Juliet and to Tom, Alice and Mike.

CONTENTS

To facilitate the cross-reference, the names of all surviving distilleries are printed in bold type throughout the book. The index on page 120 identifies the main reference page for each distillery.

ACKNOWLEDGEMENTS

I am extremely grateful to everyone in the Scotch Whisky industry who has given me help at every stage in the research and preparation of this book. I have visited every malt whisky distillery in Scotland and the courtesy and assistance given to me by everyone that I met was in every way excellent.

Individually it is impossible to thank all those people who have helped me along the way, but I must mention the invaluable help from: Patrick Millet and Elaine Bailey of Diageo; Christopher Martin of Justerini & Brooks and his colleagues at Drummuir Castle; Jim Cryle of Chivas Brothers; Neil Boyd of John Dewar & Sons Ltd; whisky writers Wallace Milroy and Helen Arthur; Phillipa Ireland and Derek Brown of Glenturret distillery; Christine Logan

of Morrison Bowmore Distillers; Mark Reynier and Jim McEwan of Bruichladdich distillery; and, for his special help in clearing a log jam, Sir George Bull.

The owning companies of the distilleries have provided many of the illustrations in this book. For their time and resourcefulness in providing illustrative material I am especially indebted to: Christine Jones of Diageo plc; Bill Bergius of Allied Distillers Ltd; Hugh Morison of the Scotch Whisky Association; Matthew Mitchell of Morrison Bowmore Distillers; Colin Ross of Ben Nevis Distillery; Rebecca Richardson of Glenfarclas Distillery; Yvonne Thackeray of Chivas Brothers Ltd; Elodie Teissedre of William Grant & Sons Ltd; and Jacqui Stacey of Inver House Distillers Ltd.

Opposite: Edradour distillery in 1930.

CHAPTER ONE

SCOTLAND'S MALT WHISKY INDUSTRY — AN INTRODUCTION

Of the 730 distilleries legally registered during the last two hundred and thirty years to make single malt Scotch whisky, just eighty-eight survive. Nine can trace their origin to the eighteenth century, sixty-six to the nineteenth century and thirteen began production in the second half of the twentieth century.

Scotland's Malt Whisky Distilleries traces the origin and the life of each distillery alive at the beginning of the twenty-first century. It is the story of a unique industry that has over five hundred years of history. The Scotch whisky industry has survived astonishingly well whilst exposed to the ravages of time. It has been subjected to crippling harvest failures; government interference; wild, punitive and often unreasonable increases in excise duty; wartime restrictions on production; the temperance movement; Prohibition; economic recession; mergers and takeovers; and the inevitable interference of the company finance director.

Our story begins in 1775 when **Glenturret**, the oldest of our surviving distilleries, was established and ends in 1995 when **Isle of Arran**, the youngest distillery, was completed. A third of the sixty-six distilleries to have survived from the nineteenth century were built in the euphoric years of the 1890s. Bust followed boom with the calamitous crash in 1898 of Pattison's, a firm of whisky blenders based in Leith. No new distilleries were to be built for nearly sixty years. Whisky-making was banned in the war years of 1917 to 1919 and again from 1942 to 1944. After the end of the Second World War, such was the development of the worldwide love of Scotch whisky that in 1974 more whisky was made and sold than in any year before or after.

The malt whisky industry is based on three of nature's most natural ingredients: barley, yeast and water. It is an industry with the simplest of origins, quite literally emerging out of the farmer's back yard where his small crudely-made still was used to convert surplus barley into alcohol and then sold to friends and neighbours for ready cash.

Governments soon realised that taxing *uisge beathe*, the water of life, was a good source of revenue to line their coffers and to help pay for wars and other absurdities, and so excise duty was imposed on the size of stills and the spirit that was produced in them. This stimulated many distillers to go underground, quite literally in many cases, and make their whisky illicitly.

Following the Excise Act of 1823, the industry that we see today began to take shape and was increasingly operated on a legal basis. Geographically, distilleries were built in areas where water was in abundance, where barley was readily available, and peat or coal could be found to malt the barley and heat the stills. There are records of hundreds of legal distilleries registered before and after the 1823 Act, but few of those early distilleries survived for more than a few years. In the County of Perthshire there are records of around one hundred distilleries licensed in the late eighteenth and during the nineteenth centuries. Their average life was eleven years and only four – **Glenturret**, **Aberfeldy**, **Edradour** and **Blair Athol** – have survived to this day.

In the early days of whisky-making the market for whisky was very local to the distillery and then the distillers found that with some effort they were able to interest the urban markets of Scotland's growing industrial central region in the joys of drinking good Highland malt whisky. In the second half of the nineteenth century, with the invention of the Coffey patent still and the production of grain whisky, the blended whiskies that were made by mixing malt and grain whiskies took England by storm and, in due course, the rest of the world.

Distilleries have flourished in many parts of Scotland. Today's picture is a very different one from that of the 1870s. Two regions have notably waxed and waned in their importance. The Lowland

Right: Laphroaig distillery.

area of southern Scotland and the town of Campbeltown in the Mull of Kintyre in the south-west are now shadows of their former selves. The Speyside region of the Highlands grew in the 1880s and 1890s and knocked the other two regions off their perch by producing a style of malt whisky favoured by the blending companies.

The whisky industry has been a major contributor to the Scottish economy for many years and, with annual worldwide sales of over one thousand million bottles, the export value exceeds £2.3 billion. It is a unique industry in having stocks amounting to seven years' future sales maturing in some of the coolest, damp, remote, windswept sites in the world. All of it stored in oak casks and all of it evaporating a share to the Angels at the rate of nearly two per cent every year!

Vast fortunes have been made and lost in the making of whisky. There have been great personalities and characters that have played key roles in the boom and bust of the industry. George Smith, Peter Mackie, Alexander Edward, Charles Doig, James Barclay, Joseph Hobbs, the Pattison brothers, Sam Bronfman, William Grant and of course, the whisky baron families of Dewar, Haig, Walker and Buchanan have all played significant roles in shaping the complex business we have today.

Huge companies have emerged to become key players in the business. The largest, Diageo plc, owns twenty-seven distilleries. Strong formidable international brands have evolved over the last hundred years. Based on the consistent quality of the malts in the blends, the international brand names that have stood the test of time include Johnnie Walker, Dewar's, Teacher's, White Horse, Black & White, J&B Rare and Haig. In the last twenty or thirty years the same international success story has been unfolding for an

SQUAREING THE "JOHNNIE WALKER" BOTTLES

increasing number of successful single malt Scotch whiskies, notably **The Macallan**, **Glenmorangie**, **Cardhu**, **Glen Grant**, **The Glenlivet** and **Glenfiddich**.

It is an industry that today still employs the same principles of making whisky as it did two hundred years ago. It is now however no longer the hand-crafted cottage industry but it has evolved into a highly efficient production process. Over recent years there have been a number of new strains of barley and the efficiency of each new one is measured at the end of the distillation process by its ability to yield increasingly larger amounts of litres of pure alcohol (lpa) than the one it replaced. Where a dozen men were needed fifty years ago to carry out the processes of mashing, fermentation, distilling and cleaning of the equipment, one man can now do this using his computer terminal from the comfort of his chair. During the last forty years there have been some radical changes in the distilling processes carried out on site. In the 1960s most distilleries gave up the malting of barley. Large industrial maltings produce barley malted to the distillers' exacting requirements. A few of the smaller distilleries do not even mill the barley; they buy in ready-milled grist. By the early 1970s most distilleries had given up shovelling coal to heat the stills and had turned to oil or gas to provide a more convenient and efficient source of power. The oil crisis of the 1970s concentrated the distillers' minds to the more efficient use of energy. There are a few in the industry of today who may wish to forget how, in the 1960s, several exotic ways were devised to use the surplus heat and hot water produced in the distilling process. It is said that the need to breed and rear trout, salmon or eels and to grow orchids or tomatoes often dictated the programme of distilling!

Opposite: *Over a hundred years of advertising has played a huge role in making Johnnie Walker the largest-selling blended whisky in the world. Johnnie Walker's unique square bottle was the ideal subject for an early twentieth-century advertisement drawn by W. Heath Robinson.*

Right: *Elegant stills at Bowmore, one of Islay's seven distilleries.*

Coopering, the making and repair of casks, is now rarely carried out at the distillery. In the last twenty years the number of trained coopers has fallen from one thousand to less than four hundred. An increasing number of distilleries now no longer mature the spirit that they produce on site. They send the new spirit by road tanker to be filled into casks and then stored in a central warehousing complex. Interestingly, there are a few instances where the spirit is matured in an entirely different area of Scotland from where it is made.

Whole communities have grown around the distilleries. There are many examples of several generations of the same family having worked in the same distillery. A few distilleries, because of their remoteness, have in the past had to establish a social infrastructure of houses, and perhaps a school and community centre, in order to attract employees and their families. The closure of a distillery threatens the whole *raison d'être* of this type of community. This was the case when **Bunnahabhain** on Islay closed in 1982 and **Ardbeg**, also on Islay, closed in 1996.

Every distillery is unique with its own identity and distinctive character. A few have managed to remain almost unchanged in outward appearance since Victorian times. Campbeltown's **Springbank** probably has the honour of bowing least to the pressures of modernity and only makes changes and improvements when absolutely necessary. Chunks of it are positively Dickensian and the whisky is none the worse for that! **Edradour** distillery in Perthshire comes a close second. In the most idyllic of locations, it is a classic example of how the original farm-based distilleries would have looked in the early years of the nineteenth century.

Many of our surviving distilleries have suffered from some abominable modernisation. Much of this took place in the years leading up to the boom years of the early 1970s when there was an urgent need to boost production capacity. Most of the character of the Victorian stone-built buildings was obliterated or demolished and replaced with a bland concoction of concrete, reinforced steel, harl and glass.

A nineteenth-century print of Bowmore showing the method of transferring casks and other cargo between the distillery and ship in the days before the town's jetty was built.

Spirit safes at Longmorn distillery, near Elgin.

Most distilleries are to be found in rural areas. A few started life in rural areas but have been absorbed by towns and their suburbs or, as in the case of **Oban**, the distillery became the nucleus of the town that was built around it. Most of the island distilleries were built next to the sea and used small coastal ships to bring in barley, coal and empty casks, and then to despatch the full casks of whisky. Many of the distilleries built in the late nineteenth century were deliberately located to enjoy the benefits of being close to the growing network of railways.

Within the distilleries there is a great range of distilling equipment. Some of it is surprisingly very old, in some cases dating back to the late 1800s. The skill of the specialist craftsmen, the coppersmith, the carpenter and the cooper is everywhere to be seen. The shape and size and the beauty of the copper stills can be overwhelming to any visitor. There are 445 stills in our eighty-eight distilleries, and they are all different! The quality of workmanship in the making of mash tuns, huge wooden wash backs, the stills and the copper and brass spirit safes is inspiring.

When the distillation is complete, the spirit is finally put to rest and matured in casks made exclusively from oak. A large cooperage on the road between Craigellachie and Dufftown in Speyside welcomes visitors to witness the impressive traditional crafting by the coopers of casks that will be used and re-used to mature whisky for at least fifty years.

There is a more than a hint of superstition and fear in the distilleries. After many years of using wooden wash backs made from pine or larch, dare the distiller replace them with those fashioned in stainless steel without risking an unwanted change in the whisky when it will be ready for drinking in ten or so years' time? It was a brave man who decided to replace the worm tubs at a Speyside distillery. The effect on the spirit produced was so significant that a few years later the condensers were replaced with traditional worm tubs. When stills are replaced or repaired, the coppersmith is instructed to copy precisely every dent from the old to the new for fear that the slightest alteration in design will affect the quality of the spirit. One distillery manager would not remove the cobwebs in the still house lest the character of the spirit would be affected and another insisted on playing his bagpipes in the warehouse to

Detail of the painting on Wash still No.2.

guarantee the magical ingredient that made his whisky so special!

No industry can escape the realities of other competitive forces. In the early days of our story, both gin and brandy were major competitors in England. The great opportunity for the development of whisky occurred in the 1860s when phylloxera, a nasty root-eating bug, devastated French vines and wrecked the wine and brandy industry. Scotch whisky neatly stepped in to fill the gap.

There has long been a nervousness and concern about the acquisition of parts of the Scotch whisky industry by foreign companies. The first non-Scottish owner of a distillery was W. & A. Gilbey, the London-based wine and spirit merchants. Seeing the increasing popularity of Scotch whisky in England, they bought three Speyside distilleries – **Glen Spey** in 1887, **Strathmill** in 1895 and **Knockando** in 1903 – and then it was the turn of the Americans who bought their first distillery, **Dalwhinnie**, in 1905. After Prohibition in the United States ended in 1933, one American company and two from Canada made serious efforts to buy distilleries and whisky stockholding companies. Today, with a third of the malt whisky production capacity in responsible foreign ownership, the fears and concerns of last century have largely disappeared.

More than forty distilleries willingly open their doors to over one million visitors each year. Visitors from around the world marvel at the beauty of the stills and recoil with intoxicated surprise when inspecting and sniffing the fermenting wort. They are mesmerised by the weird and special language used to describe the making of the spirit, which only after spending a minimum of three years in cask can legally be called Scotch whisky. They are mystified by '*worts* and *wash*', '*feints* and *foreshots*', '*low wines* and *middle cut*'. Confusion abounds with '*draff* and *pot ale*', '*grist* and *spent lees*', '*lyne arms* and *worm tubs*', '*rummagers* and *butts*' and, above all, the '*Angel's share*'!

The Scotch whisky industry is, as we will see in the chapters of this book, a remarkable industry and it has established an enormous resilience to outside pressures and influences. It is a great story of the survival of the fittest and each one of the eighty-eight distilleries, however large or small, has its own unique story of survival.

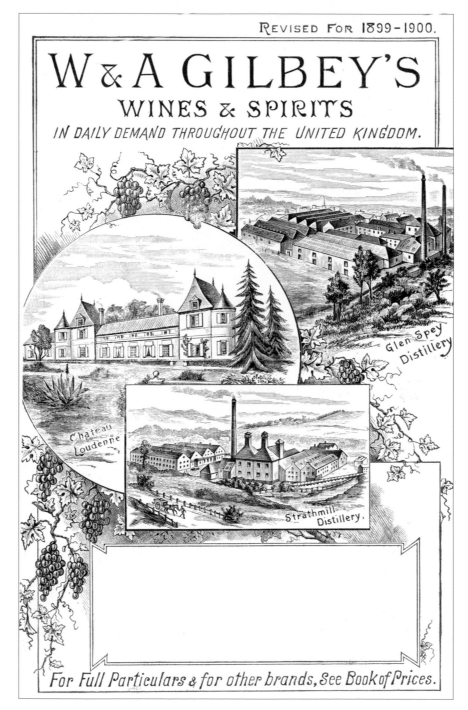

W. & A. Gilbey's trade advertisement from 1899, four years before they bought their third distillery on Speyside, Knockando.

CHAPTER TWO

THE MAKING OF
SINGLE MALT SCOTCH WHISKY

Using only malted barley in the pot still process, a single malt Scotch whisky can only be the product of the one distillery where it is produced. As with all Scotch whisky it must be matured in oak casks in Scotland for a minimum of three years. In practice many single malts are matured for at least ten years.

There are three other main categories of whisky made in Scotland. When a number of malt whiskies from several distilleries and of different ages are blended and bottled the product is called a *vatted* malt. In recent years there has been a growth of interest in producing vatted malts to satisfy a small part of the whisky market that wishes to buy a style of malt whisky where price is perhaps more important than origin.

Grain whisky is made from malted barley and other unmalted cereals in a *Coffey* or *patent* still in a process that is both continuous and efficient. Neil Gunn in his classic book *Whisky and Scotland* published in 1935 describes a patent still that produces the 'silent spirit' as it was once known, as 'an affair of two tall columns, heated by steam, into which wash is poured at one end and out of which pure alcohol pours at the other'.

The first patent still was developed by Robert Stein in 1826 and four years later an Irishman,

Aeneas Coffey patented a superior version which was soon in widespread use. Today there are eight grain whisky distilleries in Scotland and they account for about two-thirds of all whisky made in Scotland. These large distilleries are very industrial in their appearance and tend to be functional rather than aesthetic and rarely attract visitors!

Grain whisky has some slight character in taste and requires less time to mature than most malt whiskies. By law, grain whisky must be matured in oak casks and for a minimum period of three years. Grain whisky's main value has always been as a blending agent although there are a few examples of bottled single grain whisky, notably Cameron Brig and Invergordon.

Nineteen out of every twenty bottles of Scotch whisky consumed throughout the world are bottles of *blended* whisky. There are many brands of blended whiskies and there is a long list of those that have enjoyed success including the five largest global brands to have survived the extraordinary trading conditions of the twentieth century: Johnnie Walker, J&B Rare, Ballantine's, William Grant's and Chivas Regal. The Master Blender of each blended whisky aims for long term consistency and single grain whiskies are chosen with the

In 1853 Andrew Usher, The Glenlivet's agent in Edinburgh, produced a blend of Glenlivet, other malts and grain whisky. 'Old Vatted Glenlivet' is believed to be the first branded blend of whisky and sold well in Britain and throughout the British Empire.

Right: Two examples of the copper makers' plates on old distillery equipment.

Far right: Balvenie is the only distillery on Speyside to have kept the traditional malting floor

same care as the single malts that are put together to produce the final blend. Most blends are made up of at least thirty different single malts and several grain whiskies. The combination of malts and grains is usually a closely-guarded secret and although the proportion of malts to grains is rarely divulged it is generally taken to be in the ratio of 30-35% malts to 65-70% grains. Some of the more expensive premium blends can be expected to have in excess of 50% malts in the blend.

It is possible to distill all the year round, although until the 1950s when improved methods of the storage of barley were developed, the period of distilling was between October and May. The summer months, when the distillery is not operational, is known as the *silent* or *off season*. This was traditionally the period when the previous autumn's barley supply would have been exhausted and the water supplies were less certain. With the cattle grazing outdoors in the summer months there was no ready market for the draff. It was also the period for maintenance within the distillery and when the peats were cut.

There are six stages in the making of single malt whisky: **Malting, Milling, Mashing, Fermentation, Distillation** and **Maturation**.

Malting

The purpose of malting the barley is to prepare the starch in the barley grain for conversion during the mashing process into active malt sugar known as maltose. To change barley into malt involves encouraging the barley to germinate and then at the right moment, by heating the barley, to stop that germination.

The skill of malting barley was developed in the many farm distilleries that were the backbone of the industry in the eighteenth and early nineteenth centuries. The tradition was continued in most distilleries into the second half of the twentieth century. By the 1960s distillery owners realised the benefits of centralising the malting of barley and following the closure of many of the individual distillery maltings the large commercial maltings produced barley malted to the distiller's precise requirements. Floor malting of the barley lives on in only five distilleries. The two mainland distilleries to do so are **Springbank** in Campbeltown, which malts all its requirements, and **Balvenie** on Speyside; **Bowmore** and **Laphroaig** on Islay and **Highland Park** on Orkney also do so.

To produce malt in the traditional way on floor maltings is an expensive process requiring both space and manpower. It is a luxury however that is afforded by the few who zealously retain the practice in the belief that the final whisky produced is all the better for the extra effort and cost. The very best varieties of barley are used in the making of malt whisky. In recent years the varieties that have found favour with distillers include Optic, Dercardo, Chariot, Decanter and Golden Promise. Distillers seek barley low in moisture content and with a low level of protein. When the barley is brought in to the distilleries it has to be stored carefully at the right temperature and humidity to avoid the risk of infestation by insects. After being *screened* (cleaned of such foreign matter as small stones) the barley is placed in a concrete or wooden tank or trough known as a *steep*.

Water, at an ideal temperature of 16°C, is added and the barley is subjected to spells of saturation over a period of between two to three days. The period in the steep varies according to weather conditions, the type of barley used and the time of the year. After a period of saturation the water is drained from the barley which is allowed to rest damply for a while. This procedure is repeated two

A rare example of a steep barrow.

or three times encouraging the grains of barley to begin to germinate. The drained barley is then placed in heaps, or *couches* on the malting floor. The temperature of the barley slowly rises and it is spread out on the floor to a depth of about a foot. Traditionally the barley was moved from the steep to the floor in *steep barrows* with their characteristic large wooden wheels. The germinating barley takes in oxygen and gives off carbon dioxide and wooden shovels, known as *shiels*, are used to turn the barley regularly. This *turning of the piece* aerates the barley keeping the temperature close to an ideal 16°C and preventing the growing roots from becoming hopelessly entangled. During the period of malting the barley is steadily spread out further on the floor until it is finally at a depth of three to four inches. The time taken to malt the barley depends on both the time of year and the ambient temperature and can vary between five and twelve days. During germination the complex molecules of starch, cellulose and protein inside the husk of the barley are broken down to a state where they are soluble in water. The barley secretes enzymes, notably diastase, which act as important catalysts later on in the process.

The skill of malting barley is to judge when to halt the process of germination. This is deemed to be at the stage when the rootlets are about an inch long and the shoot, or acrospyre, has grown to about three-quarters of the length within the kernel. The barley is now known as *green malt*. Germination of the barley must be stopped and in those few distilleries that still carry out the process they transfer the *green malt* to be dried in the *malt kiln*.

With a moisture content of about 50%, the green malt is spread evenly to a depth of between one and two feet over the perforated metal floor of the kiln with a fire of coke or anthracite beneath. Depending on how much peat flavour is required in the whisky that is eventually produced, an appropriate quantity of peat is added to the fire at the early stage of *kilning* the green malt. The peat smoke produced in the kiln is called the *peat reek*. The open ventilator above the kiln draws up the hot air from the fire below and the green malt sitting on the perforated floor absorbs small amounts of the peat smokiness. The drying malt is dug over occasionally to ensure it is evenly dried and the kiln temperature kept below 65°C in order that the enzymes converting the starch to sugar in the grain are not destroyed. The malt becomes increasingly dry during its thirty to sixty hours in the kiln with moisture content falling to about 3%. The malt is then stored for the next stage: mashing. Although still very similar in appearance to the new barley that arrived fresh from the barley merchant it is now dry, friable, crisp and aromatic, ready to add its very special characteristics to the whisky it will sire.

A few distilleries have used a labour-saving method of malting barley devised in the late nineteenth century by the French engineer, Charles Saladin. A surviving example of the *Saladin box* system was installed in 1951 at **Tamdhu** Distillery on Speyside to replace the original floor maltings and it provides all of **Tamdhu's** needs. Consisting of a series of large concrete or metal trenches with perforated floors air is circulated through the germinating barley to control its temperature. The malt is regularly turned by means of large mechanical screws that move up and down the length of the trenches and the process takes five days. At **Tamdhu**, the *green malt* is transferred to a modern pressurised kiln to dry the grain.

Most of the malted barley in the industry is produced in the commercial maltings located in Moray, Fife, the Lothians region and at the old Port Ellen distillery on Islay. The barley is germinated in large vessels, each with a capacity of up to 500 tons, where the

Above: *Laphroaig distillery. This peat fire will dry eight tonnes of barley in the kiln above for a full eighteen hours and then, to complete the malting of the barley, warm air will be used for a further twelve. (One metric tonne equals 1,000 kg).*

Right: *Peat smoke escaping beneath the pagoda roof atop one of Laphroaig's two kilns.*

Left: *In constant use for over fifty years, there are ten of these Saladin boxes at Tamdhu each holding twenty-two tonnes of barley.*

Right: *Speyburn distillery's unique drum maltings. There are six of these Henning's drums which, when in use between 1897 and 1968, were driven by a twelve-horse-power steam engine.*

malt is turned mechanically. Where required peat-flavoured air is drawn into the centre of the drum and the malt is dried speedily under pressure. A drum malting system was installed at **Speyburn** distillery in 1897. The equipment survives to this day, but has not been in use since 1968.

Milling

The malt is *dressed* to remove the rootlets. The *combings* are sold as *malt culms* for cattle feed. The malt is then given a period of rest and stored in malt bins for four to six weeks prior to being milled.

When required for mashing, the malt is milled in a roller mill. Replacing the traditional stone grinding method the roller mill was in general use by the 1880s. Apart from a few milling machines imported from Germany and Switzerland the industry is reliant on Porteus and Boby milling machines. Manufactured in England, many mills, with minimum maintenance, have faithfully done their job for 30, 40 or more years. Using a series of rollers the mill grinds the malted barley into *grist*, a coarse flour of a consistent texture with a proportion of fine flour, *middles* (pieces of kernel, to produce the extract) and chopped husk (to aid drainage in the *mash tun*). The proportion varies slightly between distilleries and the general rule is 10% fine flour, 70% middles and 20% chopped husks. The objective is to produce a mixture that is easy to mash.

Mashing

After milling, the grist is stored in a malt *grist hopper* to await mashing. In the *mash house* the grist is fed with water under pressure through a large pipe, the mashing machine, into a large round vessel called a *mash tun* made from stainless steel or cast

Far left: *Springbank's Porteus malt mill. Through a series of rollers, batches of malted barley are milled into grist.*

Left: *A Porteus mill at Cardhu distillery.*

Below: *Taking nearly thirteen tonnes of grist, Bunnahabhain's mash tun is one of the largest in the industry.*

Bottom: *Eight o'clock on a Monday morning sees the first mash of the week at Deanston. The mash tun is one of the few in Scotland to have no cover and to retain the traditional system of revolving rakes.*

iron. In most distilleries the mash tuns are totally enclosed vessels with a perforated floor above the base.

Water at around 68°C is added to the grist. The mixture is stirred continuously by revolving rakes to maximise the extraction of sugars. The starch in the barley has at this stage been converted to fermentable sugars. The sugary liquid known now as *wort* or *worts* is drained through the perforated floor into a container known as an *underback* or a *worts receiver*. A second water, at a higher temperature of 75-80°C, is added to the porridge of *grist* and again a sugary solution is extracted and drained off. A third hotter water, at 90-95°C, is added to this low sugar-content porridge. This final water is drawn off into a tank to be used as the first water in the next mash. A few distilleries believe in adding a fourth water to extract even more of the residual sugar and then to use both the third and fourth waters as the first water of the next mash.

The exhausted grist known as *draff* is removed from the mash tun and sold as cattle food.

In many distilleries the traditional cast iron mash tun has been replaced with a German Lauter stainless steel mash tun common in the brewing industry. There is a modified version of this, known as a semi-Lauter, which until recently was manufactured in Elgin.

Left: *Traditional oregon pine wash backs at Bowmore on Islay. Only the top third of the wash back is visible.*

Top: *Glenrothes distillery. There are many stainless steel wash backs in use today. They are efficient and easy to maintain but lack the aesthetic looks of their wooden predecessors!*

Above: *Glenallachie's wash backs are unusual in both their colour and being lined with corten steel.*

These are believed to give a better rate of extraction achieved by treating the mash more gently than the traditional tuns with their spinning rakes thrashing the grist.

Fermentation

The *sweet wort* is piped through a heat exchanger into the *tun room* and directly into large covered larchwood, Oregon pine or stainless steel vats or tubs called *fermenting vessels* or *wash backs*. The wooden wash backs – the largest have a capacity of up to 60,000 litres – can have a life of forty or more years. Yeast is added to the wort and over a period of at least 48 hours the yeast will convert the malt sugars into a light crude alcohol, carbon dioxide and flavour compounds. This liquid is now called *wash*. The temperature of the wort before fermentation depends on the planned length of fermentation. For a long fermentation of up to 100 hours the wort will be put into the wash back at a temperature between 14°C and 17°C. For the more usual period of 48 to 60 hours the initial temperature will be between 18°C and 20°C. During fermentation the temperature rises and when the temperature exceeds 32°C the yeast is killed and fermentation ceases.

The effect of the yeast during fermentation can be very dramatic and the wash froths vigorously. In the early days men and boys would be employed to reduce the excessive frothing using long birch or heather *switches* or *flails*. Today's wash backs are fitted with mechanical rotating arms called *switchers* which break down the froth (the *barm*). In those distilleries equipped with stainless steel wash backs, which are sealed units, the carbon dioxide is collected from the wash backs and vented into the atmosphere.

The wash, now with a strength of about 7% alcohol by volume (abv), is pumped to a *wash receiver* or *charger*, prior to being distilled.

There are three main designs of stills. On the left of this diagram the wash still is of the lantern style. Note the steam coils in the base of the still that heat the wash and persuade the vaporised alcohol to rise up the swan's neck over into the lyne arm and through the condenser. The right hand spirit still, with a boil pot above the base, also has a steam coil and kettles that heat the low wines and again after some effort the vapours of alcohol make the journey up and over the neck and down the lyne arm to the condenser.

Distillation

The true alchemy of the distilling art lies in the pot still house. Here the very apparatus is almost primeval with the great swelling globular stills piping off to a dwindling spout that pierces the wall. These shapes must be amongst the most ancient recognisable to civilised man.

Land of Scotch, Alastair M. Dunnett (Scotch Whisky Association 1953).

Malt whisky is distilled in pear-shaped copper pot stills. Every distillery has at least one wash and one spirit still. **Glenfiddich** boasts twenty-eight.

The first distillation of between five and six hours takes place in the wash still. The wash is boiled from within the still by steam filled coils and as alcohol has a lower boiling point than water (78.5°C), the alcohol is vaporised. The vapour first rises to the neck of the still, then passes into and down the *lyne arm* to the condenser, where the alcohol vapour is cooled and liquefied. Sixteen distilleries retain the original form of condenser, a coiled copper pipe known as a *worm*, which sits in a tank of running cold water. The alcoholic product of this first distillation, or *run*, is known as *low wines*. It is impure and at a strength of 25% abv it is stored in a *low wines receiver* or *charger* awaiting a second distillation.

Since the 1970s most of the stills which previously had been heated directly by coal fires were converted to being heated indirectly by steam coils within the lower part of the still. This was not a new invention, the first steam coils were used at **Glenmorangie** in the 1880s. The traditional method of direct heat from coal fires beneath the stills was until recently employed in **Glenfiddich** and at **Ardmore** distilleries. The only distillery to use coal-fired stills is the recently reopened **Glendronach**. **Glenfarclas**, **Macallan** and fourteen stills at **Glenfiddich** use a gas flame directly applied to the base of the still. To prevent the burning of the heavier solubles that gravitate to the base of the wash still a mechanical *rummager* is fitted inside the still. This is a rotor arm with chains attached that regularly clear any solubles that have attached themselves to the inside of the lower part of the still.

The residue after the first distillation is a waste liquor of high protein value. Known as *burnt ale* or *pot ale* or *spent wash* it is converted along with the draff from the mashing process into *dark grains* for animal feeding, or alternatively it can be evaporated to produce a syrup.

The low wines are distilled for a second time in the spirit or low wines still and this can take between six and eight hours. The purpose of this second distillation is to concentrate further the alcoholic content of the low wines. The entire product of both distillations passes through the *spirit safe* where the stillman regularly checks the strength of the distillate. The first part of the run of the second distillation is very strong and impure. This is the *head* or the *foreshots* and is returned to the low wines charger. The middle part or *middle cut* of the run is what the stillman is seeking. This is the *heart of the run*, the new spirit or *new make* that will soon be filled into casks for maturation. The spirit is piped to the *spirits receiver* and has an average strength of about 68% abv. This middle cut can be up to 40% of the spirit distillation, although in a few distilleries it can be as little as 15% of the run. Towards the end of the second distillation the heavier elements in the low wines will vaporise and reappear as unwanted *feints* or *tail* or *aftershots*. The feints, along with the foreshots, are returned to the low wines charger and will be used along with the next distillate from the wash still as the next charge for the spirit still. The residue in the still, *spent lees,* has no use or value.

The invention of the spirit safe is attributed to Septimus Fox in the early 1820s. Its use was made compulsory in the 1823 Legal Act, although its general use in the industry was not until two years later. The spirit safe is a brassbound glass tank through which flows all of the spirit from the stills. The safe contains hydrometers and thermometers for testing the spirit and a handle on the outside of the safe connected to a swiveling spout within the safe is used by the stillman to direct the flow of the spirit to the low wines or spirits receiver.

Bunnahabhain. Access to a still is through a firmly secured man door in the side of the base of the still.

The lyne arm, *lye pipe* or *spout* leading out from the still's *swan neck* towards the condenser can vary greatly in thickness and length. The rake of the angle of the lyne arm is a significant factor in the style of spirit produced. The closer to the horizontal the more likely the heavier alcohols in the distillate will run back into the still and be redistilled. This is termed the *reflux*. Refluxing is an important aspect of the distillation process. As the alcohol vapours rise up the swan neck, some vapours will cool and condense before they can be collected. They will fall back into the still and are redistilled. This gives the spirit-to-be more exposure to the copper of the still and it is a general rule that the more contact with copper the lighter the spirit. In a number of distilleries, a small condensing unit known as a *purifier* (or *rectifier*) is fitted in the lyne arm to increase the reflux by condensing some of the vapours in and near the neck and returning them to the still.

In tall stills such as at **Glenmorangie** some of the vapours condense well before they can escape the still and again they are redistilled and a lighter spirit is thus produced.

Triple Distillation.
Traditional Lowland distilleries use a method of triple distillation using an extra *intermediate still*. The low wines are produced as

Opposite above: *Macallan's small stills have surprisingly long and fat lyne arms leading down to their condensers. It is a sturdy spirit that is produced through these stills and well prepared for maturation in sherry casks for many years.*

Opposite below, left: *Tormore's wash stills have lyne arms leading from the swan's neck into rectifiers that encourage the vapours of alcohol to return to the stills for a further distillation. Eventually the lighter style of alcohol makes the journey to the condenser and if selected by the stillman as the middle cut the spirit is directed to the spirit receiver for filling into casks for maturation.*

Opposite below, right: *There are some wonderful examples of the skill of craftsmen in our distilleries. This spirit safe at Dalmore is a fusion of copper, brass, lead and glass created to have a legal function and an entry in the competition for the Turner prize!*

Left: *These are Dalwhinnie's answers to condensers. Two very substantial worm tubs cool the distillate of the distillery's two stills.*

Below: *A constant supply of cold water from the distillery's burn feeds Edradour's two old and quaint but nevertheless efficient worm tubs.*

Bottom left: *Rothes-based coppersmiths, A. Forsyth & Son Ltd, make many of the stills in Scotland's malt whisky distilleries. After years of use, sections of the stills become thin and have to be replaced. These old stills are waiting to be recycled.*

Bottom right: *A magnificent example of the coppersmith's skill is seen hanging above the low wines and feints receiver at Orkney's Highland Park distillery.*

Casks awaiting the attention of the twenty coopers at Taylor's Speyside Cooperage near Craigellachie.

usual in the wash still and sent forward to the intermediate still. From this distillation the distillate with a strength above 20% is sent forward to the spirit still for a third distillation. The middle cut from this distillation is of a higher strength than in the normal two still distillations with spirit collected at 81-87% abv. It is a lighter spirit, maturing to become charactcristically a clean-flavoured and fragrant whisky. From the distillation in the intermediate still, the distillate below 20% is recycled with the next batch of low wines for distillation in that second still.

In the still house all the pipes are colour coded and have been since 1824.

Wash is in **red** pipes, *low wines* and *foreshots* are in **blue** pipes, *new spirit* in **black** pipes and water in **white** pipes.

Maturation

It has taken twelve to fourteen days to change the simple barley grains into the complex spirit that will not legally be called single malt Scotch whisky until it has matured in an oak cask with a capacity no greater than 700 litres for at least three years.

In *Whisky and Scotland* Neil Gunn says 'the maturing of whisky is a natural slow process, during which an ethereal aroma is developed and the pungent taste of the new spirit gradually disappears giving place to a mellowness and flavour that suggest body without loss of cleanness to the taste. To listen to the silence of 5,000 casks of whisky in the twilight of a warehouse while the barley seed is being scattered on neighbouring fields, might even make a Poet Laureate dumb'.

Richard Grindal, in more recent times wrote in his book *The Spirit of Whisky*, 'the transformation from fiery, crude and unpalatable new make to smooth, mellow spirit is one of nature's miracles'.

After distillation, the new and colourless *make* (spirit) is collected in a *spirits receiver* where it is *cut* (diluted) to a strength of around 63.5% abv by adding spring or demineralised water before being filled into oak casks. The careful selection of good casks is a very important factor in the successful maturation of

Inside the Speyside Cooperage, the team of coopers and apprentices make and repair 100,000 casks every year.

spirit. Most casks in the Scotch whisky industry have been used before to mature bourbon, whisky, sherry or port and come in a variety of sizes:

Gorda	600 litres (known as 'fat ladies')
Pipe	500 litres (port)
Puncheon	500 litres
Butt	490 litres (sherry)
Australian wine hogshead	300 litres
Hogshead	250 litres (also known as a remade hogshead or Dump hogshead – the 'hoggie')
American Barrel	180, 190 & 200 litres
Barrel	127 litres
Kilderkin	82 litres
Quarter Butt	45 litres (Firkin)
Anker	40 litres
Octave (one-eighth butt)	22.5 litres

The most commonly used cask in the whisky industry is the American barrel made of American white oak that is characteristically of low porosity. American law does not allow the re-use of the casks that have been used for maturing Bourbon. The casks are shipped to Scotland and many are remade with larger cask ends thus increasing their capacity from 200 to 250 litres. The Spanish casks used in the sherry trade are equally of low porosity and more generally available as hogsheads and butts. One in every twenty-five casks used in the malt whisky industry is a sherry cask.

Whilst maturing, the spirit changes in character and draws colour and flavour from the cask. The colour depends on the style of the cask and the length of time in which the spirit is matured.

During the process of maturing there is a loss of spirit. Known as the *Angels' share* it can be as high as 3% in the first year and 1-2% in subsequent years. The rate of evaporation slows down with time and a whisky that survives for forty or fifty years will not have suffered from total evaporation! The environment in which maturation takes place is a significant factor in the size of Angels' share. The size of cask is important. The smaller the cask the greater the percentage of loss through absorption, transfusion, exposure to damp or cold or heat, and therefore the whisky in it matures, and can eventually deteriorate, at a faster rate than whisky in larger casks. In a damp warehouse, for instance on the moist western island of Islay, with only a small range of temperature variation between summer and winter, the whisky will lose strength but maintain most of its bulk. Maturing in the drier environment of Speyside, with its warm summers and quite cold winters, strength is less affected but bulk will be lost.

The traditional manner of stowing casks is on wooden rails – *dunnage* – three casks high on earth floors. Modern purpose-built warehouses can store casks up to twelve layers high on sturdy steel racking. The larger companies have built enormous centralised warehousing complexes in the areas of distillation.

A few companies have experimented, and in their belief successfully, with block storage of casks stored on their ends on pallets six pallets high. This improves warehouse efficiency and it is said not to have any detrimental effect on the taste or quality of the whisky.

There is no simple answer to the question 'When is a whisky at its most mature and ready to drink?' Given that the spirit is initially good and filled into a good cask, different malt whiskies from different distilleries will reach perfection at different times. Neil Gunn's view was that after fifteen years in wood, whisky as a rule begins to deteriorate. Richard Grindal points out those malt whiskies with a fuller flavour, such as those from Islay and Speyside, tend to take longer to be at their best (between twelve to fifteen years of age), whereas the milder Highland and Lowland whiskies usually reach their peak in ten years.

Traditional dunnage warehousing at Glenturret in Perthshire. Only a few of the fifty different species of oak are suitable for coopering. A good oak cask must prevent seepage yet the contents must breathe and the flavours improve with time.

CHAPTER THREE

SCOTLAND'S
MALT WHISKY REGIONS

There are four main regions in Scotland where single malt whiskies are produced. The largest by far both in terms of land area and present-day production is the Highland region, and the next largest is the island of Islay. The Lowland region and Campbeltown are the smallest regions, being mere shadows of what they were a hundred years ago.

The classification of the malt whisky regions has always been on a geographical basis and the simple Highland/Lowland definition is to this day based on the Wash Act of 1784 that drew a formal distinction between the two regions for the purpose of *differential excise legislation*. In simple terms this is a line on the map connecting Greenock in the west with Dundee in the east. Highland is to the north of the line and everything to the south is defined as Lowland.

The Highland region can be subdivided into five sub-regions. The main concentration of malt whisky distilleries is in the area of the valley of Scotland's second longest and fastest flowing river, the Spey, and its tributaries the Livet, Avon and Fiddich. This is Speyside, with its core area the 'Golden Triangle' centred on the towns of Rothes, Elgin, Dufftown and Keith. The Greater Speyside area includes distilleries on or near the rivers Lossie, Findhorn and Deveron and two distilleries on the Moray coast. The other four sub-regions of Highland are Northern, Western, Eastern and Southern.

Islay is a region in its own right with its own special taste characteristics and unique historical identity. There are good reasons for including Scotland's other island distilleries alongside Islay and grouping **Highland Park** from Orkney, **Talisker** from Skye, **Tobermory** from Mull, **Jura** and **Arran**, into an enlarged region of Islay and other islands.

There are generally agreed characteristics of the malt whiskies produced in each of the four regions.

Over half of Scotland's malt whisky distilleries are to be found in one region within Highland. Speyside is the heart of whisky distilling in Scotland. Its whiskies are quite sweet, somewhat complex and sophisticated with finesse, elegance and some fruitiness and they are very much favoured by blenders. Most are lightly peated with some smokiness and, when matured in sherry wood, they can have a chocolatey richness.

Whiskies from the Northern region are usually medium-bodied, quite complex but somehow delicate. They are usually dry, with a hint of spice and salt. The Eastern Highlands produces medium to full-bodied smooth, sweetish whiskies with a dry finish. They are often malty and slightly smoky, sometimes fudge-like with spice flavours. From the Southern Highlands whiskies tend to be lighter, somewhat fragrant with heather and honey on the nose, but with a dry finish. The few Western whiskies tend to be peated and rounded.

Peat covers more than a quarter of the surface of the island of Islay and all the distilleries are built on the coast. Islay malts are renowned for their phenolic, iodine seaweed-like qualities. They are the strongest flavoured of the Scottish malts. They are also the weightiest, most heavily peated and most pungent and are used with care when blending. Other Island whiskies vary, each having their own character. Usually peaty, but less so than Islay, with some salty maritime influence.

The triple distillation method, which produces a lighter style of whisky, was traditionally used in the Lowland region. They are the lightest of the malts both in colour and weight and they are not influenced by the sea or peat. Typically they are generally fragrant and floral with some fruity notes and a dry finish.

A malt whisky from Campbeltown has been described as above Highland and below Islay in terms of heaviness. With three quite different styles being made at **Springbank** and the recent haphazard history of production at **Glen Scotia**, it is difficult to pinpoint the current style of a Campbeltown.

As to the joy of tasting, Neil Gunn wrote in 1935:

Single malt whiskies, with their individual flavours, do recall the world of hills and glens, of raging elements, of shelter, of divine ease. The perfect moment for their reception is after arduous bodily stress, or mental stress, if the body be sound. The essential oils that unwind in the glass then uncurl their long fingers in lingering benediction and the nobler works of Creation are made manifest. At such a moment, the basest man would bless his enemy.

CHAPTER FOUR

WHISKY'S UNEASY HISTORY

The first duty on spirits was imposed by the Scots Parliament in 1644. The Treaty between Scotland and England, the Act of Union in 1707, provided for the same duties to be levied on excisable liquors in both countries. The earliest reliable date of any record of whisky production in Scotland was 1708 when just over 50,000 gallons of malt whisky were made. The distillers at that time were mainly farmers who were distilling any barley surplus to their needs. For many years there was friction between the farmer distillers who made the whisky and were unwilling to pay tax to the excise men whose duty it was to collect it. Illicit distilling was rife. For over 120 years many laws were introduced to discourage illicit distilling. Duties were levied on the content of stills and the amount of wash produced. There were rules governing the minimum size of stills and there were different rules and levels of duty depending on whether the distillery was located in the Highlands or the Lowlands.

The early years of the nineteenth century were especially difficult for farmers with a number of wet cold summers and poor harvests. The authorities totally banned distilling in seven out of the first fifteen years of the century. Instead of euphoria at the defeat of Napoleon in 1814 there was a period of sharp economic recession. For distillers in the Highlands, new laws introduced in 1816 restricted the minimum size of a still and many small distillers were put out of business. By 1819, there were only fifty-seven licensed distilleries, with many thousands continuing to distill illegally. In 1822, over six thousand cases of illicit distilling were taken to court.

The Excise Act of 1823 gave a positive encouragement to the licensed distillation of whisky. The cost of a licence fee was set at £10 and duty on a gallon of proof spirit was halved to 2s 5d (12p). Stills had to be no smaller than forty gallons and there was to be the legal enforcement of the use of the new spirit safe. This legislation succeeded in stamping out illicit distilling and produced more revenue for the Exchequer. Tax was paid on two million gallons in 1823 and on six million gallons two years later. The number of illicit stills operating in 1823 was estimated at about 14,000 but in 1830 this number had fallen to less than 400. Legally registered distilleries opened all over Scotland and by 1825 there were 263 distillers licenced to produce whisky. In Campbeltown, a town at the southern end of the Mull of Kintyre, twenty-seven distilleries opened in the fifteen years to 1838. In the 1830s there were several years of poor grain harvests and the resulting recession caused many farm-based distilleries to close.

The development in the 1820s by Robert Stein, and a few years later by Aeneas Coffey, of the method of continuous distillation of grains was to have a huge impact on the industry. These grain whisky stills were capable of producing large quantities of relatively cheap high-strength spirit and in the latter part of the nineteenth century they were to have a major effect on the whole structure and nature of the industry.

The repeal of the Navigation Acts in 1845 freed up trade and allowed access to new markets in the Colonies. A year later, the Corn Laws were repealed and distillers were allowed to import cheaper barley and maize which was of great benefit to the grain distillers. In 1853 a change in the law allowed the 'mixing under bond of whiskies from different distillations of various years at the same distillery'.

Regular increases in the level of duty payable in Scotland meant that by 1855 duty had been equalised in Scotland and England. Consumption increased in England but this did not compensate for the sharp fall in demand in Scotland where a sluggish economy and the strengthening influence of the Temperance movement led to the closure of over thirty distilleries. Gladstone's Spirit Act of 1860 increased duty by a quarter to ten shillings (50p) a gallon and for the first time permitted whisky to be sold across the border into England in bottles rather than casks. New legislation allowed grocers to apply for an 'off' licence to sell alcohol to be consumed off the premises.

The increase in duty was to have a lasting effect in Britain for many years by reducing consumption and lowering sales. Growth in the whisky industry was to come from developing business overseas. Many Scots had emigrated and took their love of whisky with them. The Blending Act of 1865 gave an enormous stimulus to the industry by allowing the blending together of malt and grain whiskies. Many new blends were soon to emerge, individually uniform in character, milder than strong flavoured malts and therefore with a broader appeal. Initially most of the blended whiskies were sold as 'own labels' by grocers, wine merchants and brewers. It was during the 1870s and 1880s that the development plans were being put in place of the brands of blended whiskies that were destined to dominate the world markets during the twentieth century. Blends such as Dewar's, Johnnie Walker and Buchanan Blend were sold into England through offices established in London and large provincial towns. During the 1880s and 1890s the owners of these brands made some extraordinary sales journeys around the world, developing enthusiasm for their whiskies and establishing a framework of agencies and distributors.

The huge damage inflicted on the French wine and cognac business by the vine-destroying phylloxera bug gave an additional stimulus to the whisky industry. Whisky was seen as a very suitable alternative drink to cognac. The rapid growth in the rail network in Britain together with the improvement in the roads and the development of regular services on shipping routes to overseas countries, speeded up the movement of barley, coal and casks into the distilleries and the sale of whisky to customers everywhere.

All of this was against a background of peaks and troughs in the British economy. Demand for whisky was such in the late 1860s that the first malt whisky distillery for twenty years was built at **Cragganmore** on Speyside in 1869. This was followed in the early 1870s by the rebuilding and expansion of a number of distilleries and the building of a few new ones. There was a new peak in production in 1877. In the same year, a group of six of the largest Lowland grain whisky distilleries amalgamated to form the Distillers Company Ltd (DCL), an organisation that was to have a huge and often beneficial influence on the industry for at least the next one hundred years. The economy turned sour in the second half of the 1880s and this period of uncertainty encouraged amalgamation and take-over and the strengthening of links between blenders and distillers. In 1886 a number of wine and spirit merchants and several large blenders joined forces to float the North British grain whisky distillery in Edinburgh to supply the member companies with grain whisky suitable for blending.

In 1887 the purchase of **Glen Spey** distillery in Rothes by the London wine and spirit merchants W. & A. Gilbey was the first move by a non-Scottish company to acquire a foothold in the whisky industry. This was the same year that the definitive book on the distilleries, their location, history and equipment, *The Whisky Distilleries of the United Kingdom* was published. Alfred Barnard had been commissioned by Harper's *Weekly Gazette*, the wine, spirit and brewing trade magazine, to visit all of the distilleries in England, Wales, Scotland and Ireland. The project took him nearly two years and he visited 118 pot still distilleries in Scotland. It is worthwhile noting that fifty-three of these distilleries survived the pressures that were to affect the industry over the next 115 years and are still in production today.

The last decade of the nineteenth century was to be the most exciting chapter in the history of the whisky industry. To satisfy the demand from the blenders for more and more malt whisky, distilleries were rebuilt and extended and thirty-three new distilleries were built in the 1890s, of which twenty-one were on Speyside. The blenders favoured the delicate flavour of the Speyside malts. The bland Lowland malts and the strong flavours of the island and Campbeltown malts were of little interest to blenders who were increasingly supplying smooth and mellow blends to their customers. Other factors in favour of developing distilleries on Speyside were the good supplies of quality barley, peat and pure water and an efficient railway system connecting the area with the cities and ports where the whisky was blended, bottled and exported overseas.

The rapid growth in exports and the rush to build new distilleries lead to speculation and over-production. One whisky blending company was to be the cause of a very major problem to all involved in the industry. The Pattison brothers, Robert and Walter, began their business life as partners in a grocery business in Leith. In 1887 they embarked on whisky blending and converted to a public company in 1896 based, as it later transpired, on a fraudulent balance sheet. They sold mainly to the domestic market and their whisky was heavily advertised including an occasion when they sent hundreds of grey parrots around the country, each trained to squawk 'Drink Pattison's Whisky'! They forged links with whisky brokers, invested in the expansion of such distilleries as

Glenfarclas and became the largest customer of a number of distilleries, notably William Grant's **Glenfiddich**.

Robert Pattison was involved in the flotation of the **Oban** and **Aultmore**-Glenlivet Distillery Co. and from his £40,000 profit on the deal built a huge mansion. A vast warehouse and very lavishly appointed offices were built in Leith. The premises were so palatial that John Grant of **Glenfarclas** said he was urged to sing 'I dreamt that I dwelt in marble halls'. The company had borrowed heavily from several banks. Their activities were based mainly on fraud, spurious information, falsified balance sheets and payment of dividends from capital. On 6 December 1898, Pattison's suspended payment to their creditors. Their subsequent bankruptcy affected the whole industry. The problem of chronic over-stocking throughout the industry was brought to the fore. The country was awash with surplus stocks of whisky. The Pattison brothers were jailed for fraud and no new distillery was to be built for the next sixty years. The whisky bubble had burst.

The first decade of the twentieth century saw the death of Queen Victoria, a significant supporter of the industry during her long reign, and the end of the Boer War that was followed by a period of economic recession. Whisky sales declined in the domestic market and, although the hangover of post-Pattison stocks was slowly being corrected, a fifth of the distilleries had closed by 1910. There were however encouraging and welcome signs for the whisky industry with increased export sales to the United States, Australia, South Africa and Canada.

During the same decade there was considerable debate over the legal definition of whisky. The two main points key to this debate were the minimum proportion of malt in a blend and the minimum maturation period. A Royal Commission was established to hear all sides of the matter but sidestepped the two main issues by concluding that 'both patent grain whisky and pot still malt whisky qualify as Scotch whisky'!

1909 saw Lloyd George's 'People's Budget' in which he raised the duty on spirits by a third. The price of a bottle of whisky rose to half a crown (12½p). This was believed by many to be the death knell of the whisky trade in Britain. Demand fell sharply and twenty-two distilleries closed in the next three years. There was continued activity by the major companies, notably DCL, in trying to persuade the industry to avoid over-production during such a

Left: The size and extent of the scandal and financial failure that followed the collapse of Pattison's in December 1898, marked the end of the most discreditable chapter in the history of the whisky trade.

difficult period. A further savage blow to the Scotch whisky industry was when the First World War broke out in 1914. This brought the threat of another punitive budget from Lloyd George who had said, 'Drink is doing more damage in the war than all the German submarines put together'. His proposal to double the rate of duty met with great opposition from the industry. He was persuaded to compromise and accepted a proposal from the distillers that the planned increase in duty was replaced by a ban on the sale of whisky under three years of age. The immediate effect of this legislation was the closure of fifty blending and distribution companies and the DCL took every opportunity to buy distressed stock and companies that had a good export business.

The Government banned all pot distilling between June 1917 and March 1919. The distilleries had only just re-opened after the war when the United States imposed a period of Prohibition which was to last until 1933. The effect, however, on the Scotch whisky industry was not as drastic as was at first feared. There was a highly organised illicit trade through Canada and islands in the Caribbean and a small quantity of **Laphroaig** and a few other whiskies were imported legally into the United States because of their medicinal qualities.

The 1920s was a period of rationalisation with the DCL becoming increasingly influential in all sections of the industry. Having expanded to include the 'Big Five', (Dewar's, White Horse, Johnnie Walker, Black & White and Haig), DCL fully represented all interests of the Scotch whisky industry with its original core grain distilling interests, many of the largest blending companies and an increasing number of malt whisky distillers. In 1925, Scottish Malt Distillers (SMD) established eleven years earlier with the merger of five Lowland malt whisky distilleries (including Rosebank, St. Magdalene and **Glenkinchie**) merged with the DCL. In 1930 DCL put all of its twenty-three malt distilleries under the aegis of SMD. DCL's influential role was vital in the bitter years of economic recession in the early 1930s and was well positioned to lobby a government that was indifferent to the plight of the industry and other industries dependent on it. By 1933 the production side of the whisky industry had deteriorated to such an extent that only two malt whisky distilleries were in production that year. The economy slowly recovered in the years immediately after the Great Depression but the outbreak of war in 1939 dashed all hopes of

Right: *Advertising Johnnie Walker Red Label to the wartime readers of* The Sphere *had a theme of encouraging the war effort. This subject by the marine artist Frank Mason was published at the time when all distilleries were closed.*

Good work . . . Good whisky

JOHNNIE WALKER
Born 1820 — still going strong

any benefit that may have been enjoyed by the Scotch whisky industry.

War brought higher duties and with the need to improve dollar earnings, the industry was encouraged to concentrate on export and to restrict sales within the domestic market. The Government initially rationed supplies of barley for distilling purposes but by 1942 had decided that there would be no further distilling. By October of that year all distilleries were closed. It was to be a full two years later towards the end of 1944, when limited supplies of grain were again made available for distilling on condition that more of the industry's stocks of mature whiskies would be made available for export. Thirty-four malt distilleries opened in the first few months of 1945 and in April a further stimulus was given to the industry in Churchill's famous minute, 'On no account reduce the barley for whisky. This takes years to mature and is an invaluable export and dollar producer.' It took until December 1953 before the Government ended its direct control of the production levels of the Scotch whisky industry and a further six years before stocks of maturing whisky were in line with demand and only then could rationing by means of a quota system be discontinued.

More distilleries came back into production and, during the 1950s, the developing global demand for whisky stimulated a number of distillery owners to re-equip and expand their production.

The first entirely new distillery to be built in sixty years was **Tormore** on Speyside that began production in 1960. The growth in demand continued apace during the 1960s and SMD embarked on a programme of expansion increasing by a half the number of stills in their distilleries in the period 1959 to 1967. Over the same period malt whisky production soared from sixteen million to over fifty million gallons and the demand for 'Scotch' in the American market trebled between 1960 and 1968.

The early years of the 1970s saw the boom continue and 1974 was to be the peak year of production. The global economy suffered as a result of the oil crisis in the mid-1970s and for a few years so did the whisky industry. A total of twelve distilleries were built between 1960 and 1975 and of these ten have survived into the twenty-first century. A modest recovery at the end of the 1970s led to the building up of maturing stocks and an over-enthusiastic view of the future prospects of the industry once again led to over-production. Drastic corrective action was necessary and DCL made

the painful decision to close eleven of its distilleries in 1983 and a further ten in 1985. Production was drastically reduced in their other distilleries by working 'three day weeks' and by extending their silent seasons. Other companies closed distilleries and went on to short-time working. The problem of production running ahead of demand was never far away during the last years of the twentieth century. The key factor to a stable relationship between production and demand is to maintain an industry level of around seven years of maturing stocks.

During the twentieth century there have been huge changes in the structure of the industry and the ownership of the distilleries. DCL grew dynamically in the first half of the century and had long been a strong influence in the industry until swallowed by Guinness in 1986. Now owned by Diageo, it operates twenty-seven distilleries and accounts for about one third of all malt whisky production. In the 1970s, three brewery companies, Scottish & Newcastle, Whitbread and Allied Breweries, with a desire to supply their pubs and off licenses with their own whiskies, developed a taste for buying brands of blended whisky and owning a few distilleries. Allied Distillers, as the company is now known, has evolved as a major global force in wines and spirits and retains its distilling interests. For the other two brewery companies, their involvement in distilling was a passing phase. Ten distilleries remain truly independently owned, surviving because of the single-minded approach of their owners and their individual character making them unique in their own right.

Serious attempts by foreign companies to buy into the Scotch whisky industry began in the 1930s when Hiram Walker of Canada bought Ballantine's whisky and two Speyside distilleries. In 1949 Seagram, another Canadian company, put in its first appearance when they bought the long-established blenders, Chivas Brothers of Aberdeen and Chivas Regal, which was to become a leading global brand of blended whisky. To support their sales Seagram's built up a collection of nine distilleries, all on Speyside. Companies followed their move into Scotland from France, Japan, the United States, Luxembourg, Bermuda and, for a brief period, Spain. In the year 2000, Seagram surprised the whisky industry by selling by auction all of their interests in wines and spirits. By the end of 2001 the French company Pernod Ricard were the new owners of all Seagram's Scotch whisky interests.

During 2001 there were two other significant changes in ownership of Scotch whisky distilleries and brands. Whyte & Mackay, which had been part of an American company since the early 1990s, was brought back into Scottish ownership following a management buyout. This MBO marks the end of direct North

Opposite: *The first malt whisky distillery to be built in the twentieth century was Tormore, which opened in 1960.*

American ownership of any part of the Scotch whisky industry. A new owner of Inver House Distillers was announced during 2001. A Thailand-based company, the Great Oriole Group, bought the company and its clutch of five distilleries and controls them through its UK subsidiary, Pacific Spirits (UK) Ltd. In December 2002, CL Financial Ltd, the Trinidad based drinks group that owns Angostura Bitters, bought Burn Stewart Distillers and its two distilleries, **Deanston** and **Tobermory**. Today, about a third of all malt whisky is produced in distilleries owned by foreign companies.

The malt whisky industry has entered the new Millennium in good condition. The fittest have survived the rigours of the past and most are highly efficient with established customers for their whiskies either as single malts or for use in blends. The growth of worldwide interest in malt whiskies has never been stronger. There is, however, a cloud that is never far from the horizon of the long-term prospects of blended whisky. A number of the older established markets have been in decline during the last ten to fifteen years and the lost volume has been replaced by growth in sales to new markets in Europe, South America and Asia. The potential for finding new markets for blended whiskies is diminishing and the competition in the form of new and alternative drinks is increasingly more intensive.

There can be no doubt that the future for Scotland's malt whisky distilleries will not be easy, but as it will be seen, it never has.

CHAPTER FIVE

THE DISTILLERIES:
1775 TO THE PRESENT DAY

1775 GLENTURRET (Highland)

The outbreak of the American War of Independence in 1775 was of little relevance to the farming folk of Perthshire, one of Scotland's ancient counties to the north of Edinburgh and Glasgow.

Originally known as Hosh, the oldest surviving single malt distillery in Scotland was built in that momentous year and it has survived with some difficulty and a lot of luck for over two hundred and twenty-five years. Its snug, almost secret, location in a fold of the foothills of the Highlands is one of those classic areas where illicit distilling flourished. Hosh was however set up as a legal distillery and the founding Drummond family kept it going for its first seventy years and John McCallum for a further thirty. The next owner was Thomas Stewart who, in the distillery's Centenary year, renamed it Glenturret. The fine and fast-flowing River Turret that tumbles past the distillery rises in the mountainous area to the north and it is from the source of the river, Loch Turret, that today the distillery obtains its water by means of its own pipeline.

In the first thirty years of the nineteenth century, eighteen distilleries were built in the vicinity of Crieff but their average life was only thirteen years and the poor grain harvests of the 1830s and 1840s killed them all off by 1850, bar one, Glenturret.

The distillery did suffer during the great downturn in the whisky industry of the first two decades of the twentieth century. The distillery

Glenturret's small wash still is a striking piece of equipment.

closed in 1921 and when the owners, the Mitchell Brothers, were liquidated in 1929, the distillery was dismantled and the buildings were used for farm storage.

In 1957, it was the vision and optimism of one man, James Fairlie, who, with his whisky blending experience in Glasgow, sensed the need to satisfy the blenders' fast growing demands for malt whiskies. He bought and rebuilt Glenturret and in 1960 the first spirit was flowing from the distillery's two small stills and the first whisky bearing the Glenturret name was in bottle five years later. In those early days the bulk of Glenturret's small production was sold to the blenders.

The future of the distillery was uncertain during the difficult years of the 1970s and a friendship with the French drinks firm of Remy-Cointreau led to them buying the distillery in 1981. Subsequent investment in visitor facilities made the distillery one of Scotland's main tourist attractions. By 1991 over one million visitors had made the pilgrimage to Glenturret and five years later that figure had doubled. In 1990, as part of a distribution agreement between Remy-Cointreau and Highland Distillers, the owners of The Famous Grouse blended Scotch whisky, Glenturret was handed over to Highland and it joined their small collection of distilleries, safely back under Scottish ownership.

Glenturret is a distillery where one can enjoy an intimate experience with the making of malt whisky. It is small, but not quite the smallest. **Edradour**, near Pitlochry, another of Perthshire's four distilleries, has that honour. What Glenturret

Glenturret, Scotland's oldest distillery, is found just to the west of Crieff in Perthshire and is seen here shortly after it had been rebuilt following forty years of closure.

does have, and no other distillery has yet dared to challenge, is the legendary tale of one cat, Towser, who died in 1987. Embalmed in the *Guinness Book of Records* for her serial killing of 28,899 mice during a remarkable career spanning twenty-four years, Towser has long been a star attraction at the distillery. She is omnipresent with her own statue where the visitor must pay appropriate homage

and in the distillery shop every type of souvenir can be bought bearing her glorious image.

Let us hope that this, the oldest and almost the smallest distillery, finds within Towser's immortal memory the same ingredient for survival as the ravens have provided at The Tower of London. In 2002, Glenturret distillery took on the dramatic role as the spiritual home of The Famous Grouse, with its new Famous Grouse Experience visitor centre promising its patrons 'the world's most innovative whisky experience'. With a small annual production of an unremarkable malt whisky, this new role for Glenturret will bolster the chances of Scotland's oldest distillery surviving for many years into the future.

The Famous Grouse

Matthew Gloag & Son Ltd was established in Perth in 1800 as a grocers and wine merchant. In the 1860s blended whiskies were added to the firm's range of wines and other spirits. In 1898 one of these blends was named The Grouse Brand and its local popularity led to it being re-styled as The *Famous* Grouse. During the second half of the twentieth century the UK has had a succession of popular brands of blended whisky. Haig, White Horse, Johnnie Walker Red Label and Teacher's have each had their day. For the last twenty years the popularity of Bell's has been a challenge to The Famous Grouse. It was during the 1970s, after Highland Distilleries had bought Gloag's business in Perth, that the brand soared to be the largest selling whisky in Scotland, and it still holds that position. Grouse's growth in popularity in England and Wales was in the 1980s and early 1990s. Overall the 'low flier', as it is affectionately known (along with not-so-affectionate Cockney version of 'Mickey Mouse') is the second largest brand in the UK. Exporting Grouse was not a major priority of the company until the 1980s. Total worldwide sales now exceed two million cases.

The Famous Grouse is a classic case of how to develop a successful brand in the modern competitive domestic and world markets. It has grown slowly and steadily and has skillfully avoided many of the pressures and pitfalls of conforming to defined marketing rituals. The advertising copy line for years was 'Quality in an Age of Change' and The Famous Grouse justly deserves whisky writer Jim Murray's accolade when he describes it as 'A quite brilliant blend'.

THE FAMOUS GROUSE

FINEST SCOTCH WHISKY

100% SCOTCH WHISKIES BLENDED & BOTTLED BY

Matthew Gloag & Son Ltd.,

1779 BOWMORE (Islay)

Established on the very edge of Loch Indaal by a local merchant John Simson, Bowmore is the oldest legal distillery of the seven surviving distilleries on the Hebridean Island of Islay. It has had a long and successful history with little interruption of production apart from during the Second World War when the Air Ministry requisitioned Bowmore and used it as a Coastal Command operations centre and base for flying boats giving anti-submarine assistance to Atlantic shipping convoys.

Little more than a century earlier in 1837, William and James Mutter, Glasgow merchants of German extraction bought Bowmore. They used their own 145-ton ship, SS *James Mutter*, to bring in empty casks, coal and barley, and to take whisky to Glasgow and their warehouses built in the archways beneath the city's Central Railway Station. Bowmore had no pier and the ship had to anchor a little way off shore and horse-drawn carts were used to haul the cargo to and from the ship. This was no easy task in the gale-force winds regularly encountered in this west-facing loch.

Bowmore became a renowned malt whisky in several export markets and by the end of the nineteenth century the distillery was producing over a million litres of whisky in a year.

The distillery had three subsequent owners before being bought by Stanley P. Morrison Ltd in 1963. In 1994, the Japanese company Suntory which had had a financial interest in Morrison's for a number of years, took full control of Bowmore and the company's two other distilleries, **Auchentoshan** and **Glen Garioch**.

Bowmore and **Laphroaig** are the two distilleries on Islay that preserve the traditional way of malting some of their own requirements of malted barley. Bowmore's floor maltings provide a third of the distillery's needs.

The distillery is impressively smart in appearance both externally and within. There is a magnificent copper and brass mash tun, six Oregon pine wash backs and four elegant stills. Even the casks are presented in their very best coopered condition. The process water for the distillery is from the River Laggan, some five miles

GLOAG'S PERTH WHISKY

"DALMORE"

FINEST OLD SCOTCH.

ESTABLISHED IN 1800   *Matthew Gloag & Son,*
Perth.

Above: *It was a slow process to bottle whisky before the advent of fully automated bottling machinery. Fifty years ago it took nine employees of Matthew Gloag's to bottle, fit a closure, label, inspect, wrap and pack the precious whisky into a wooden box.*

Above right: *It was commonplace in the middle of the last century for whisky merchants to bottle a cask or two of a range of single malt whiskies and to sell them to their wholesale and retail customers.*

Right: *It is little suprise that some whiskies taste of the sea! Casks waiting to be filled are stored close to Loch Indaal at Bowmore and then for the next ten years or more they will be stored in warehouses built on the water's edge.*

distant. It is delivered to the distillery by means of a nine-mile conduit, or as known locally, a *lade*.

Nothing is wasted at Bowmore. A special waste-heat recovery system is used to provide hot air during a major part of the kilning stage of malting the barley. Excess energy is used to heat the water in the town's community swimming pool built in the distillery's No.3 warehouse, gifted to the town in 1990.

The spirit of Bowmore is matured in sherry and American oak casks and a variety of styles is produced ranging from the medium-bodied fresh tasting Bowmore Legend through several different ages and styles until one reaches the very complex 21, 25 and 30-year-old expressions.

1786 STRATHISLA (Highland-Speyside)

For over 160 years Keith's first legal distillery was known as Milton. For many years however the whisky made at Milton was known as Strathisla.

In 1786, Milton's first legal distiller was George Taylor, a banker, postmaster and a prominent figure in the local flax and linen industry. When William Longmore bought the distillery in 1830 he set about updating and expanding the distillery, which in spite of a destructive fire in 1876 and an explosion in the malt mill three years later, flourished under his ownership. In 1870 the distillery was renamed Strathisla and this was to last until 1890 when the name was again changed back to Milton. Longmore died in 1882 and the business continued as William Longmore & Co. Ltd, the first Highland whisky firm to become a limited liability company.

During the Second World War, London financier and Russian-born impresario Jay Pomeroy, whose previous name was Joseph Pomerantz, bought the distillery. At the time of his purchase of the distillery large amounts of Milton's whisky stocks were sold at very low prices. The Inland Revenue claimed unpaid tax of £360,000 and three years later Pomeroy was found guilty of tax evasion and fined over £110,000. The distillery had been neglected and was in a bad state of disrepair. Pomeroy's private company was wound up and went into receivership.

In the few years between the end of Prohibition and the start of the Second World War, Canadian and American drinks companies took a keen interest in investing in the success of the Scotch whisky industry. One company that was to become a powerful influence in the industry in the second half of the twentieth century was the Canadian firm of Seagram, headed by Samuel Bronfman. His first move into the industry was to arrange with DCL to secure a supply of malt whiskies to be used in the blends that he sold in Canada. In 1935 he bought a Glasgow firm of whisky merchants with its large stock of fine aged malt whisky. After the war his next move was the purchase in 1949 of the Aberdeen whisky-blending house of Chivas Brothers. This was to become the jewel in the Seagram crown, because the purchase included Chivas Regal, a brand of blended whisky that had before the war established a large following in North America. Bronfman was helped greatly in his endeavours to secure his first moves into Scotland by a friend of many years, Jimmy Barclay. Barclay had entered the industry as an office boy at **Benrinnes** distillery in 1902. He then moved to Glasgow and worked for Sir 'Restless' Peter Mackie of **Lagavulin** and White Horse fame. After a period as a director of Hazelburn distillery in Campbeltown, Barclay set up on his own account as a whisky broker and merchant. He travelled widely in North America during the period of Prohibition and chalked up considerable sales with his many 'rum-runs'! It was whilst he was a director of Chivas Brothers that Barclay alerted Bronfman that the business was for sale. With Chivas Brothers safely in his hands, Bronfman's plans for the revitalisation and eventual relaunch of Chivas Regal as a 12-year-old meant that he needed his own reliable sources of whisky making. Barclay paid £71,000 at the public auction in April 1950 to secure the purchase of Seagram's first distillery in Scotland, Milton.

Immediate steps were taken to overhaul and renovate the dilapidated distillery and it was renamed Strathisla in 1951. In 1965 the distillery was extensively enlarged and two new stills were added to the existing pair. The wash stills are of the traditional lantern style, whilst the spirit stills are of the ball type to encourage reflux and the production of a light spirit.

Strathisla is one of Scotland's most beautiful distilleries retaining much of its traditional appearance. It produces a big and elegant malt, some available as a 12-year-old single malt and most of it is matured for at least twelve years to be at the heart of the Chivas Regal blend.

Above: *An old whisky jar from the early 1900s confirms that Strathisla whisky is from William Longmore's Milton distillery.*

Right: *A postcard from 1953 shows Strathisla very much as it is today – neat, compact and retaining many of its traditional features.*

Chivas Regal

Chivas Brothers, established in Aberdeen by brothers James and John Chivas, can trace its origins as far back as 1801. Royal Glendee and Royal Strathythan were their first and most successful blends and they were well established by the 1880s with the brands achieving considerable export success by the end of the century. The Chivas family connection died out in 1893 and the manager and the master blender Charles Howard carried on the business. It was he who in 1909 had developed the remarkable blend, Chivas Regal, initially as a 25-year-old vatted whisky and mainly sold to the North American market.

Following a fire in 1929 in the Aberdeen premises and the death of two of the partners in 1935, the business was sold a year later to a consortium including Stanley P. Morrison and then again in 1949 to the Canadian company, Seagram. This acquisition became the focal point of the development of the Seagram Scotch whisky empire, eventually acquiring or building nine distilleries, all of them on Speyside. Following the sale of Seagram's wine and spirit business in 2001, Pernod Ricard of France now owns Chivas Regal and all of Seagram's whisky interests.

Chivas Regal was relaunched as a 12-year-old in the American market in 1952 with the advertising slogan, 'Scotland's Prince of Whiskies'. Today it is a hugely successful brand with annual sales of nearly four million cases.

1790 BALBLAIR (Highland)

John Ross began distilling at Balblair farm in 1790 and by the 1820s he was producing over 2,200 gallons of whisky in a year, most of it sent by horse and cart to Cromarty and then shipped to Leith for sale to customers in Edinburgh and Glasgow. Around 1872 the distillery was expanded and, by the time of Alfred Barnard's visit in 1887, the distillery's annual production had risen dramatically to over 50,000 gallons. The tenancy of the distillery remained in the Ross family for over 100 years until 1894 when Alexander Cowan, a wine merchant from Inverness, took out a sixty-year lease on the distillery. The new terms of the lease specified that Cowan had to build a new distillery within a year on a two-acre site, half a mile from the existing distillery. This was successfully achieved and when the new Balblair was completed the old one fell into disuse. The distillery was built adjacent to the railway and coal and barley were brought in and whisky was sent out to the blenders.

The 1909 'People's Budget' brought hard times on many distillers and Balblair suffered to such an extent that Cowan was sequestrated in 1911 and the distillery was closed. It took a long twenty years to sell off the maturing stocks of Balblair. The distillery was taken over by the army for the duration of the war. Balblair was part of the Balnagowan estate and following the

Far left: *An advertisement that appeared in 1954 in the American magazines* Town and Country, Fortune *and* Holiday *announces that Chivas Regal is Scotland's Prince of Whiskies.*

Left: *One of the first orders in 1953 destined for Chivas Brothers Import Corporation of New York being carefully assembled and packed into wooden crates.*

Situated in a very attractive setting near Dornoch Loch, Balblair retains much of its traditional appearance.

bankruptcy of the estate in 1941, the freehold of the distillery was for sale. After being out of production for 36 years, Robert Cumming, a Banff solicitor, bought Balblair and production resumed in 1949.

Cumming retired in 1970 and sold the distillery to his main customer, Hiram Walker of Canada. Balblair had become a key malt within their increasingly successful Ballantine's blend. Following Hiram Walker's merger with Allied Vintners in 1987, the distillery returned to British ownership. The whisky industry was in a state of overproduction in the early 1990s and Balblair was a candidate for 'mothballing' by its new owners. It survived this possible ignominy by being sold to Inver House Distillers in 1996 and was thus added to their increasingly interesting portfolio of distilleries.

Starting life as a very simple farm distillery, Balblair has over time been expanded but it has not lost anything of its earlier charm. It is very attractively situated above Dornoch Loch where the burns run down from Struie Hill to water the farmlands of the Edderton, known locally as the 'parish of the peats'. The malt whisky from Balblair is both complex and satisfying, combining a sweet start with a dry finish.

1794 OBAN (Highland)

Oban was a mere fishing village when brothers John and Hugh Stevenson established the Oban Brewery Co. A year later, in 1794, distilling was first recorded and the first license to distil was dated

Stafford Street and M'Caig Tower, Oban

The town that grew around Oban distillery almost starved it of life and possible future growth. The special role as Classic Malt's 14-year-old representative of the Western Highlands has secured the future of this charming distillery seen here in an old postcard of the 1920s.

1797. The Stevenson family was responsible for the planning and development of the town of Oban and for the next twenty years concentrated on housebuilding, slate quarrying and boat building. Their interest in distilling was revived in 1818 and the business remained in family hands until sold to a local merchant, Peter Cumstie, in 1866. In turn he sold on to John Walter Higgin in 1883, who rebuilt the distillery in the early 1890s. Higgin sold the distillery in the boom year of 1898 to a consortium of whisky merchants and blenders, which also owned the Speyside distillery, **Aultmore**. They struggled to keep the business afloat and in 1923 Oban was sold to John Dewar & Sons Ltd of Perth and two years later the company became part of DCL.

The future of the distillery was still not secure. Oban is a small distillery and it could not be expanded because of its cramped position between the steep cliffs behind and the town's main street in front. The distillery was closed during the 1930s and again during the war years and yet again in 1968. In 1972, when there was a lot of optimism regarding the future of the whisky industry and the need to expand production, DCL rebuilt the still house and gave the distillery a new lease of life. In 1989 Oban was selected to represent the West Highland region as one of the range of six Classic Malts. It now boasts a fine and popular visitor centre built in the old floor maltings which had been closed in 1968.

Oban is unique for a mainland distillery in having been built very close to the sea. It is also unusual in having the distillate from the distillery's two lantern-shaped stills cooled through worm tubs rather than the more usual condensers. A very lightly peated malt, the Oban 14-year-old Classic Malt has a fruity nose, a spicy sweetness and with smoke and some salts it has a long drying finish.

1797 GLEN GARIOCH (Highland)

With the closure in the 1980s of Glenugie distillery in Peterhead and Glenury Royal in Stonehaven, Glen Garioch became the most easterly of Scotland's malt whisky distilleries. Located in the small town of Old Meldrum a few miles inland from Aberdeen in the fertile, well sheltered and highly cultivated valley of the Garioch, Barnard in his 1887 visit described the area as the 'Granary of Aberdeenshire'.

Established in 1797 by Thomas Simpson, the distillery had a succession of owners until 1884 when J.G. Thompson & Co. of Leith acquired it. In 1908 ownership transferred to the Glengarioch Distillery Co. Ltd, whose Managing Director was William Sanderson,

of VAT 69 fame. Sanderson's merged with Booth's (Gin) Distilleries in 1935 and in 1943 the company became part of DCL.

In 1968 because of an inadequate water supply DCL closed the distillery. Two years later Stanley P. Morrison the Glasgow-based firm of whisky blenders and brokers bought the distillery, put down a deep well in an adjacent field and having found a reliable supply of water, expanded the distillery and reopened it in 1973. Waste heat from the distillery was used to heat greenhouses that covered an area of nearly two acres. It is believed that in one year the yield of tomatoes exceeded 180 tons! In 1982 the distillery became the first to convert to North Sea gas and with improved methods of waste heat recovery, the greenhouse experiment was discontinued in the early 1990s.

Shortly after Suntory of Japan took over Stanley P. Morrison in 1994, the distillery was mothballed and by December 1997 the warehouses cleared of stocks. The closure was short-lived and the distillery was reopened in August 1997 and in June 2000 the warehouses were also reopened.

The distillery has a very solid traditional appearance with the fine granite buildings having worn well in their long history. Unfortunately the visitor facilities have not been re-opened since the distillery's closure in 1995. Glen Garioch distillery had been host to as many as 30,000 visitors in a year.

1798 BLAIR ATHOL (Highland)

John Stewart and Robert Robertson established Aldour distillery on the Allt Dour – the burn of the otter – in Pitlochry, Perthshire in 1798. The business did not survive the high duty burden and the distillery fell silent. John Robertson revived it in 1826 following the reduction of tax in the 1823 Excise Act. Re-named Blair Athol, Alexander Connacher and his family ran the distillery for over fifty years until taken over by Peter Mackenzie in 1882. Mackenzie, born in Glenlivet, the heart of whisky country, operated as a wine and spirit merchant in Liverpool. He enlarged and improved the distillery and Barnard commented that the distillery 'uses the finest quality of barley and the malt is dried with peat brought from Orkney'. At the peak of the whisky boom in 1896, Mackenzie built **Dufftown-Glenlivet** distillery on Speyside.

The recession of the 1930s forced the closure of Blair Athol. The Perth-based Arthur Bell & Sons Ltd bought both of Mackenzie's distilleries in 1933 but Blair Athol did not re-open until after a major rebuild in 1949, the same year that Bell's became a public company.

There is no doubt that Glen Garioch single malt was used in the VAT 69 blend in the time when William Sanderson was Managing Director of the distillery. The elegance of this advertisement is typical of the style of the early 1930s.

Blair Athol is a very distinguished looking collection of buildings and is well known to the many tourists who leave the main A9 to visit Pitlochry and break their journey to and from Inverness and the Highlands. A visitor centre was opened in 1985 and welcomes around 50,000 visitors a year.

The distillery was expanded in 1973 and again in 1982 with two additional stills and four large stainless steel wash backs to work alongside four fine larch wash backs. Using unusually hard water flowing from Ben Vrackie, Blair Athol 12-year-old has a sweetish taste with a hint of smoke. For over a half a century it has been at the heart of the Bell's blend.

Bell's Extra Special

In 1840, Arthur Bell joined Thomas Sandeman, a wine and spirit merchant established in Perth in 1825. He worked for Sandeman for eleven years before establishing his own whisky business in 1851 with James Roy as a business partner. Arthur Bell appointed the first regular Scotch whisky agent in London in 1862 and sales of the company's whiskies made steady gains.

Scotch Fir was the first brand to be registered by the company in the 1890s. Arthur Bell forbad any form of advertising and use of the Bell name on labels was not to be seen until after his death in 1900. The first such label was for 'Arthur Bell & Sons' Pure Malt Whisky' using as its main subject an illustration of a curler.

There was a period of dramatic sales growth of Bell's Extra Special whisky in the 1970s, firstly in Scotland and then in England. It succeeded Haig and then Johnnie Walker as the largest selling brand of blended whisky in Britain. Guinness bought Arthur Bell & Sons Ltd in 1985 and twelve years later a much larger Guinness, having swallowed DCL in a very acrimonious and controversial takeover in 1986, merged with Grand Metropolitan to become Diageo. Bell's Extra Special was re-blended and relaunched in 1994 as an 8-year-old and maintains its position as the largest selling blended whisky in the country.

1798 HIGHLAND PARK (Island)

Set on a lofty hillside overlooking Orkney's capital Kirkwall to the north and the grey waters of Scapa Flow to the south, Highland Park has the distinction of being the most northerly

The first label to use the Bell's name in the early years of the twentieth century.

distillery in Scotland. It is one of Scotland's most attractive distilleries and retains a very traditional approach to whisky making. The source of the water is the pool of Cattie Maggies, a short distance from the distillery. This water is unusually hard and has an inexplicable influence on the eventual taste of the matured Highland Park.

There had been illicit distilling on the site of the present distillery for many years. David Robertson is believed to have been the founder of Highland Park and to have made distilling a legal operation in 1798. He was succeeded by a number of owners until in 1888 the business passed into the hands of James Grant. He enlarged the distillery from two to four stills in 1898 and it stayed in the hands of the Grant family until sold in 1937 to its present owner, Highland Distillers. Highland Park is a distillery that has had a steady uncontroversial history with very few breaks in production and survives as Orkney's only active distillery. It has long outlived the presence of the Stromness distillery that operated in Orkney's second largest town between 1817 and 1928. Unless there is a change of direction in Allied Distillers' interest in their Scapa distillery, a very close neighbour of Highland Park, Scapa is destined to remain a silent neighbour, mothballed in 1993. Scapa has in recent years been brought back into short spells of production to maintain continuity of supply in support of its small but growing number of aficionados. Scapa's wash still is now the only remaining example of a *Lomond still* to be found in Scotland.

Highland Park distillery retains its Y-shaped solid stone floor maltings and two working kilns. The company owns its own peat beds three miles to the west on Hobbister Hill. The hill is close to the sea and the peat is cut to a shallow depth. The marine influence combined with the heathery roots of the peat impart special flavours when the peat is burned for the first sixteen hours that the barley is in the kiln. Saturated with flavour the malt is then dried for a further thirty hours using coke as fuel.

The worts produced in the stainless steel semi-Lauter mash tun are transferred to one of twelve large wash backs. Ten are made of Oregon pine and two are most unusual in being made of Siberian larch. During both world wars, the Islands of Orkney had important strategic roles and tens of thousands of Allied Forces were based on the islands. During the 1939-1945 war the fine wash

Above: *Enter this gateway at Highland Park distillery in the teeth of a gale in the middle of winter, tread carefully on the malting floor, visit the still house and then nose a cask in one of the windswept warehouses and you will know why Highland Park is truly unique.*

Right: *Scapa's wash still is the last remaining example of a 'Lomond' still.*

backs seen today were used as bathtubs by many of the Canadian forces stationed near to the distillery!

Warehouses of the traditional type, with earth floors and casks stored three-high on simple *dunnage* racks, are home to 45,000 casks. Every one of these casks is exposed during years of maturation to an atmosphere laden with salty spray from the Atlantic gales that are a regular feature of life on Orkney.

The main expression of Highland Park is the 12-year-old. It is medium bodied, exceedingly smooth with some smokiness, sweetness tinged with salt, a hint of sherry and some heather on the nose. You have guessed! This is a great malt and it is one of the author's favourites!

1798 TOBERMORY (Island)

The Isle of Mull lies off the west coast of Scotland and is regarded by many as the most picturesque of the Hebridean islands. Tobermory is the capital of Mull and this attractive town with its

A postcard from 1904 shows Tobermory distillery, houses, a chapel and the warehouse. Today the warehouse has been converted into flats and the area in the foreground has been reclaimed and used as a car park.

brightly painted buildings is wrapped around the edge of a large bay and its safe anchorage. On the western edge of the bay is Tobermory distillery. It started life in 1798 as Ledaig distillery and is the only legal distillery to have been recorded on the island. Built by a local merchant, John Sinclair, Ledaig survived until 1837 when the general economic depression forced its closure. The distillery was revived over forty years later in 1878. In 1890 John Hopkins & Co. Ltd acquired the business and in 1897 built **Speyburn** distillery on Speyside. Hopkins sold both distilleries to DCL in 1916.

DCL closed the distillery in 1930. Its warehouses were used as naval stores during the Second World War and it was to be another forty years or so before the distillery was to re-open. After some reconstruction, a consortium of Liverpool shippers, operating as the Ledaig Distillery Ltd, brought life back to the distillery. The Spanish sherry company of Domecq joined the group but the prevailing poor state of the industry forced the company into receivership in 1975. After yet another period of closure the distillery was bought by the Yorkshire-based Kirkleavington Property Co. and, trading as the Tobermory Distillers Ltd, made small quantities of whisky in 1979, 1980 and 1981, and again in each of the years between 1989 and 1992. It was during this uncertain

period that the warehouse was sold and converted into flats and the local dairy used part of the distillery to mature cheese!

In 1993 hope for a stable future of the distillery returned with new owners, Burn Stewart Distillers of Glasgow who, as whisky blenders, were already distilling at **Deanston** which they had bought in 1990 and their first move was to re-equip the distillery. The water supply from the hills above the town is sufficiently flavoured with peat as to negate any need for other than an unpeated malted barley. The link with the producers of Mull's Tobermory cheese continues with the supply of the draff to the farm's cows. The cheese is however no longer matured in the distillery and never should have been!

Tobermory's stills are very unusual in that their lyne arms are at a sharp upward angle and are bent to squeeze them into their condensers and to accommodate the arrangement of four stills in a somewhat cramped still house.

The distillery has had a chequered career with a variety of owners and has been closed or only working occasionally for almost half of its long and precarious existence. During the period of sporadic production in the 1980s, the Tobermory name was used for a blended whisky and then also applied confusingly to a vatted malt. In more recent times Tobermory has become more firmly established as a fresh, lightly peated, medium-dry, 10-year-old single malt, smooth and fruity with a lovely smoky nose.

A final surprise from this distillery is that Ledaig is still very much alive as a second single malt produced in the distillery. It is deep gold in colour, with a pronounced peatiness and with an intense taste that is rich then dry and spicy. There is no doubt that Ledaig is a true island malt and its big difference from the Tobermory single malt is the use of a strongly peated malt barley. It is made using Tobermory's mash tun and wash backs but then has exclusive use of two of Tobermory's stills to help create Ledaig's distinctive character.

Tobermory really is a 'Tale of Two Malts'!

1810 ISLE OF JURA (Island)

Jura is the strongest contender for the most remote and beautiful location of any of Scotland's malt whisky distilleries and can only be reached by your own boat or by island hopping via Islay. George Orwell lived on the island for a while and in 1948 completed his famous book, *1984*, shortly before his death. It was his landlord James Fletcher who was to be instrumental in securing the survival of distilling on the island in the late 1950s. The Isle of Jura distillery is to be found in the island's main village, Craighouse, on the edge of the sea at the southern end of the magnificent Small Isles Bay with its many tiny rocky islands.

It was founded in 1810 on a site of known illicit distilling and in 1831 William Abercrombie was its first licensee. There were a number of owners over the next forty years until, in 1876, James Ferguson & Son bought the business and set about rebuilding the distillery. By the end of the nineteenth century Ferguson despaired of the restrictive and demanding conditions imposed on him by the owners of the distillery, the Campbell family. In 1901 Ferguson stripped the distillery of its stills and other equipment and abandoned it. The roof was taken off in 1920 and the distillery became a ruin.

That would have been the end of the story for Jura's distillery if it were not for the initiative in 1958 of two local landowners, Mr Riley-Smith and James Fletcher. Jura's economy had suffered badly during the first half of the twentieth century and they believed that a distillery would be a source of new life and work for the island with its dwindling population of 150. They approached the Edinburgh firm, Scottish Brewers, and with their financial support a new distillery was designed and built by William Delmé-Evans, a farmer, architect and distiller, who had previous experience in the late 1940s designing Tullibardine distillery in Perthshire. He was also to be responsible for the design and building of **Glenallachie** distillery opened on Speyside in 1968.

The new Jura distillery opened in 1963 and from the outset it was intended to produce a much lighter Highland style of whisky far different from the heavy peaty Islay style of the original distillery. The water from the Market Loch in the hills beyond Craighouse is dark with peat but using a very lightly peated malt and tall stills the malt whisky produced is light in colour, with a delicate nose and a light body.

Through a succession of takeovers, the distillery is now owned by Whyte & Mackay.

Above: *Jura is both desolate and beautiful. From the Sound of Islay, one of the mountainous 'Paps' is visible and above the shoreline is a good example of a raised beach.*

Below: *This view across the Small Isles Bay from the Isle of Jura distillery must be the best from any distillery in Scotland. But there will be those who do not agree! Caol Ila, Bowmore, Bruichladdich, Ardbeg, Lagavulin, Laphroaig and Bunnahabhain – to mention a few near neighbours!*

1812 ROYAL BRACKLA (Highland-Speyside)

This is Shakespeare's Macbeth country. The distillery established in 1812 by Captain William Fraser on the site of a former malt brewhouse close to the River Nairn is at the extreme northwestern edge of Speyside. This part of the Cawdor estate on which the distillery is built is an area of gentle hills and open spaces of heath, broken by belts of pinewood and swept by the invigorating winds from the Moray Firth.

Fraser was the first whisky distiller to receive a Royal Warrant of Appointment, granted by King William IV in 1835 and renewed by Queen Victoria in 1838, the year after William's death.

In 1844, the Edinburgh whisky merchants, Andrew Usher & Co. were appointed sales agents for Royal Brackla and became partners in the business. It is very likely that Ushers, who were the first to practice the blending of malt and grain whiskies to produce propriet-ary brands to be sold under the blender's name as a guarantee of quality, used Royal Brackla in those first blended whiskies.

The distillery was substan-tially rebuilt in 1890 and again in 1898. After Usher's death in 1898, the distillery survived under new owners and was bought in 1925 by John Bisset & Co., an Aberdeen firm of whisky blenders who in 1943 became part of DCL.

The distillery was further developed and enlarged in the 1960s and 1970s only to be closed between 1985 and 1991 as part of DCL's programme of distillery closures to reduce the high level of stocks in the industry.

In 1997, a year after the distillery was upgraded to become a fully mechanised distillery, Guinness, owners of DCL since 1986, merged with Grand Metropolitan to form Diageo. To avoid problems of competition rules in the United States, Diageo sold the blended whisky, Dewar's White Label, and four distilleries (Royal Brackla, **Aberfeldy, Craigellachie and Aultmore**) to Bacardi, famous for its brand of white rum and already the owner of the coastal Speyside distillery, **Macduff**.

An early twentieth-century postcard of Laphroaig distillery shows two large stacks of peat and to the right of the chimney is the still house and two wormtubs.

Royal Brackla is a large, handsome, well-equipped and efficient distillery and under its new owners has begun a new and invigorated stage in its life.

It is not easy to find this malt but when you do the 10-year-old is big and intense with both smoke and sweetness.

1815 LAPHROAIG (Islay)

The southeast coast of Islay is incredibly rugged and regularly swept by the wildest of Atlantic storms. Donald and Alexander Johnston started Laphroaig distillery in 1815 on the rocky shore of Laphroaig Bay. In 1836 Walter Campbell, who owned the land on which Laphroaig was built, leased an adjoining piece of land to two financiers from the mainland, James and Andrew Gairdner, who built a small distillery called Ardenistiel. Two distillers, James and Andrew Stein were brought in to run the distillery. Ardenistiel had the same water source as Laphroaig and Johnston, concerned that there would be insufficient water for two distilleries, had a six-year dispute over the matter until, in 1846, Andrew Stein died suddenly and his brother moved to Port Ellen distillery. Attempts were made to keep Ardenistiel alive but it was not viable and during the 1860s production ceased and it was absorbed into Laphroaig.

Laphroaig remained in the Johnston family and the Hunter branch of it until 1954, when following the death of the heirless Ian William Hunter, Laphroaig was bequeathed to Miss Bessie Williamson, who had been employed in the company for over twenty years.

Distinctive and uncompromising in style, Laphroaig's oily body always reeks of peat and has a particular medicinal aroma. During the period of Prohibition, Laphroaig was legally imported into the United States as a medicinal spirit and whilst many distilleries were suffering from a big downturn in business, Hunter doubled the distillery's production capacity in 1923.

Above: *Laphroaig's maltings are right on the water's edge.*

During the 1960s, Williamson sold the distillery to the owners of **Tormore** distillery, Long John Distillers, which was then part of the American company, Schenley Industries Inc. The English brewers Whitbread bought Long John in 1975 and after expanding the distillery to house a total of seven stills, the Whitbread spirit brands and distilleries, including Laphroaig, were sold in 1990 to the present owners, Allied Distillers.

'Love it, or Hate it' is one of Laphroaig's classic advertising messages, and it says it all. At each stage of production everything is geared to achieve in Laphroaig such extremes of flavours and the most distinctive character of any single malt whisky.

Firstly the water from the River Kilbride is low in mineral content and high in peat flavour. Laphroaig uses traditional methods to malt about a third of its malted barley requirements. Islay peat is very special, being the product of salt-sprayed heather, ferns, moss and moorland grass and some seaweed. The peat used in the first eighteen hours of the thirty-hour period of the kilning process is from Laphroaig's own peat beds at Glenmachrie. A mixture is used of the first fibrous top layer with its high moss content and the older, blacker peat from the second deeper cut. The malted barley is milled in a seventy-year-old Porteous mill and after mashing and fermentation the wash is distilled firstly in one of the three wash stills and then through one of the four spirit stills. Maturation in first fill Bourbon casks in the distillery's warehouses right on the water's edge is another essential ingredient in the complicated formula that eventually produces the unique Laphroaig, little changed in its character in the 180 years of the distillery's almost continuous and successful history.

In 1994 HRH The Prince of Wales granted his Royal Warrant to D. Johnston & Co., as Distillers and Suppliers of Laphroaig Single Malt Scotch whisky. Laphroaig is the first distillery to be so honoured.

Laphroaig *is* unique and it is for you, the reader, to judge if you 'Love it, or Hate it'!

1815 ARDBEG (Islay)

In the same year in which Laphroaig was established, Ardbeg was being built on a low rocky headland on the edge of the sea a mere two miles to the east. A year later **Lagavulin** was to become a neighbour to them both, 'twixt the two.

The local farming family of MacDougall began the business and remained involved until 1959 when the company was liquidated and Ardbeg was to face an uncertain future for forty long years.

Ardbeg was the last distillery on Islay to produce all of its requirements of malted barley. The peat used in the malting process was black with very dense vegetation, cut at a depth of eight feet in an area a few miles to the north of the distillery known as Duich Lots. Ardbeg's kilns did not have fans and the trapped peat laden smoke permeated the malt, producing an extremely pungent whisky. Another ingredient that has an influence on the distinctive taste of Ardbeg is the water. As it flows down the three miles from Loch Uigeadail to the distillery this exceptionally pure and soft water picks up the colour and taste of peat.

In 1976 Hiram Walker of Canada became the owner of Ardbeg. They closed the maltings in 1980 and between 1981 and 1989 they closed the distillery and demolished three warehouses. The lack of interest and investment gave Ardbeg a sad and most forlorn look. In 1987 Allied Vintners, later to be Allied Distillers, took over Hiram Walker and thus Ardbeg. During the 1990s the distillery, which had been reopened in 1989, was producing only a fraction of its potential and it closed again in 1996 and was put up for sale. The following year the company owning **Glenmorangie** distillery bought Ardbeg and promptly reopened it. A new visitor centre has been developed in the old maltings and there has been substantial investment in both new equipment and the renovation of buildings to secure a certain future for this delightful distillery.

The distillery retains some fascinating old equipment. The malt, which is brought in from the Port Ellen commercial maltings (located in what was the old Port Ellen distillery closed in 1983), is converted to grist in a fine example of a Boby mill, believed to be at least seventy years old. The mash tun is forty years old, made of cast iron and complete with gunmetal plates and traditional stirring gear. The spirit still has a purifier built into the end of the lyne arm to divert heavier condensed alcohols back to the still for further distillation. The still is of considerable age and is unique with rivets of an unusual 'Celtic' design and the swan neck has a rare example of an overlapping vertical joint.

Ardbeg is a fascinating distillery and has survived a difficult period when permanent closure was more of a probability than a possibility. Ardbeg is no longer the sad distillery with a forlorn look

Above left: *The 'celtic' design around the rivets shown on this photograph of the original spirit still has been faithfully copied on the replacement still recently installed at Ardbeg.*

Above: *Barnard described Ardbeg's situation on the south-east coast of Islay, 'in a lonely spot on the very edge of the sea, and its isolation tends to heighten the romantic sense of its position'.*

Right: *There is a treat in store when this fine old whisky is bottled!*

and a hopeless future. It has been totally rejuvenated and exudes great optimism for the future. Ardbeg, the single malt, is distinctively pungent and the most heavily peated of the Islay malts. There is a hint of saltiness and a natural sweetness. Ardbeg is a whisky for the connoisseur.

1816 LAGAVULIN (Islay)

The rough craggy south-east coast of Islay where **Laphroaig**, **Ardbeg** and Lagavulin put down their roots within the span of just one year is locally known as Kildalton, and these three distilleries are often referred to as the Kildalton distilleries.

John Johnston built Lagavulin in 1816 on a wonderful site right on the shore of Lagavulin Bay within sight of the ruins of the thirteenth-century Dunyvaig Castle, which was later to become the stronghold of the Lords of the Isles. In the same year, Archibald Campbell was granted a licence and built Kildalton distillery adjacent to Lagavulin. It survived for only twenty years and by 1837 it had become part of Lagavulin. The distillery eventually became the property of Peter Mackie who, until 1907 had the sales agency for neighbouring **Laphroaig**. 'Restless Peter', as he was known, decided to compete with **Laphroaig** and built a new distillery alongside Lagavulin to make an exact copy of **Laphroaig's** whisky. Malt Mill distillery had its own kiln with open peat fires, two wash backs and two pear-shaped stills modeled on the design of Laphroaig's. Malt Mill shared the use of Lagavulin's mash tun. The distillery survived long after Mackie's death in 1924 and it was eventually closed in 1960. For a few years Malt Mill's pear-shaped stills were used alongside Lagavulin's two stills but were eventually replaced with stills of the Lagavulin design with their bulbous base, broad swan neck and narrow, steeply sloping lyne arms.

The soft and peaty water flows down to Lagavulin from the Solan Lochs in the hills two miles away. Lagavulin's own maltings were closed in 1974 and now the richly peated malted barley is brought in from Port Ellen maltings. After mashing the wort is fermented between fifty-five and seventy-five hours in one of ten larchwood wash backs which are over fifty years old.

The malt whisky is characteristically very dry, round and soft with mellow edges. This is the result of the unusually long and slow distillation with five hours in the wash still and nine hours in the spirit still. In 1989 the world of malt whisky drinkers was introduced to the 16-year-old Lagavulin as the Islay representative in the range of Classic Malts. It is pungent and smoky, seaweedy and intense. Lagavulin is a whisky for the devout, not for the undecided.

Above: *Another Islay distillery in a wonderful location. Lagavulin is the home to one of the six Classic Malts.*

Below: *Lagavulin in the 1940s with whisky being collected by a 'Puffer' and you are left in no doubt as to the distillery's connection with White Horse whisky.*

Above: *The message on the reverse of this postcard posted from Southern Nigeria in 1909 reads, 'We found several hundreds of these postcards in a case of whisky… so I am postcarding on the cheap today'.*

Right: *A 1928 advertisement for White Horse whisky draws the reader's attention to the new screw cap closure: 'Opened in an instant – no corkscrew required.'*

White Horse

The first link between Lagavulin and White Horse blended whisky began in 1867 when the whisky merchants, James Logan Mackie & Co. of Glasgow, bought the distillery. J.L. Mackie's nephew, 'Restless Peter' Mackie joined the firm in 1878 and made his first visit to Lagavulin in that year. In 1890 the name of the company was changed to Mackie & Co. and it was at this time that the company introduced their blended whisky originally called Mackie's White Horse Cellar Scotch Whisky.

The name White Horse was derived from an old coaching inn of that name in Edinburgh's Canongate that had been owned by the Mackie family for generations. Described by Sir Robert Bruce Lockhart as 'one-third genius, one-third megalomaniac, one-third eccentric', Peter Mackie with boundless energy and integrity developed the foundations of this major whisky company. In partnership with Alexander Edward, **Craigellachie** distillery was built on Speyside in 1891 and one point on which Mackie was most insistent was that good whisky needed a period of at least

THE OLDEST HORSE IN THE WORLD.
Incomparable whisky—Incomparable bottle. Opened in an instant—no corkscrew required

three years maturation before sale. This was indeed to become law during the First World War. Three years after Mackie's death in 1924, the company became the last of the 'Big Five' (the others being Haig, Dewar's, Buchanan and John Walker) to join the DCL. In 1926 the company introduced the first screw cap in the industry and this produced a remarkable doubling of sales in six months. This venerable brand retains a small core of followers in Britain and continues to sell in excess of one million cases a year around the world.

Left: Bladnoch, Scotland's most southerly distillery is alive again and producing up to 100,000 litres a year.

Below: An old stencil from the days when Arthur Bell & Sons of Perth owned Bladnoch.

1817 BLADNOCH (Lowland)

Situated in the rich agricultural area of Dumfries and Galloway a mile from Wigtown, Bladnoch is the most southerly of Scotland's distilleries and is one of the three surviving Lowland distilleries.

Established in 1817 by brothers John and Thomas McClelland, the distillery remained in family ownership until, after a period of six years closure, it was bought in 1911 by Wm Dunville & Co. Ltd of Belfast. Trading as T. & A. McClelland Ltd, the distillery was re-equipped and re-opened the following year. Production stopped during the war and was intermittent during the 1920s. Bladnoch ceased production in 1930 and in 1937 the company was wound up. After the Second World War Ross & Coulter, a Glasgow firm of whisky brokers, bought the distillery, dismantled the distilling equipment and in 1954 sent the three stills to Sweden. The distillery was re-opened in 1957 by A.B. Grant, Glasgow-based whisky

blenders and exporters and in 1964 Ian Fisher of McGown & Cameron, a Glasgow firm of blenders and wholesalers, became yet another new owner of Bladnoch. In 1973 Inver House Distillers Ltd, whilst part of the Philadelphia-based Publicker Industries Inc, bought Bladnoch and sold it ten years later to Arthur Bell & Sons Ltd. Another ten years on, in 1993, with Guinness (United Distillers) as the distillery's owners, Bladnoch was closed and sold the following year to Raymond Armstrong of Northern Ireland.

Although the new owner had not originally intended to re-open the distillery, he continued to operate the visitor centre that attracts in the region of 25,000 tourists each year. In 1999 Raymond Armstrong decided to re-equip the distillery and was able to produce his first new spirit in the last few days of 2000 with nine casks placed into the duty-free warehouse bearing the date 2000.

Bladnoch is a classic case of how a distillery with many changes of ownership and years of closure and uncertainty has been rescued from almost certain oblivion by the determination of one individual whose enthusiasm and optimism has placed Bladnoch firmly back on the list of surviving distilleries.

It is an attractive distillery and its exterior is little changed from Barnard's visit in the 1880s: 'The Establishment consists of a square pile of buildings erected around a court-yard'. The distillery is on the banks of the river Bladnoch and at that point it is tidal. The distillery therefore has to bring in its water supply by means of a one-and-a-half mile lade from a dam further up the river.

Current annual production from the two small stills is about 100,000 lpa. Bladnoch has not triple distilled since the 1920s, the only surviving example of that method is to be found at **Auchentoshan**.

1817 TEANINICH (Highland)

In 1817 Captain Hugh Munro built the distillery on his own Teaninich estate near Alness in Ross-shire. The early years were a struggle as he competed with the illicit distillers in the area, but after the Excise Act of 1823 and the reduction in illicit distilling the output of Munro's distillery rose dramatically. From 1850 the distillery was leased to Robert Pattison and in 1869 to John McGilchrist Ross. In 1895 the lease passed to the two partners in the Elgin firm of Munro & Cameron, John Munro, a spirit

During the period of rapid development and demand for whisky in the 1960s and 1970s, many distilleries were treated to new larger tun rooms and still houses at the expense of their previous good-looking Victorian appearance. Teaninich is a typical example of the 'functional' look.

merchant, and Robert Innes Cameron, a whisky broker. Three years later they bought Teaninich and to meet the big demand for whisky in the late 1890s they extended and refitted the distillery.

In 1904 Innes Cameron became the sole owner of Teaninich and until his death in 1932 combined the running of the distillery with that of **Linkwood** where he was Managing Director and main shareholder.

Cameron's trustees sold the distillery a year after his death to Scottish Malt Distillers. The distillery had four stills, two of these being small. Re-opening in 1946 after a closure of seven years the small stills were removed and it was not until the period of expansion in the industry that the number of stills was again increased to four in 1962. In 1970 a new distillation unit with six stills was built. It was known as the 'A' side and after the distillery was reopened, after being mothballed between 1985 and 1991, the old still house was not used again and eventually demolished. Producing over three million litres of pure alcohol in a year, Teaninich is an important producer of malt whisky used in a range of Diageo's blends.

1819 CLYNELISH (Highland)

It has been said that Clynelish distillery was born of the Highland Clearances. It was built at a cost of £750 by the Marquess of Stafford, the future Duke of Sutherland, outside the village of Brora on the north coast of the Moray Firth. A number of his tenants were evicted Highland farmers who had settled on the newly cultivated coastal land and were growing barley. He believed that the distillery would be a ready market for the grain 'without their being obliged to dispose of it to the illegal distiller'. Purpose-built as a distillery with its own farm, the draff was fed to the pigs that in turn fertilised the land on which the barley was grown. Coal from the local Brora mine was used to heat the stills. In 1821, two years after being built, production exceeded 10,000 gallons.

James Ainslie & Co. of Leith bought and rebuilt the distillery in 1896. The bad times that followed the Pattison's crash in 1898 forced the Ainslie's to sell out in 1912 to the Clynelish Distillery Co., which was partly owned by the DCL. In 1916 John Walker & Sons Ltd became part of the Clynelish story when they took a significant shareholding in the company and when Walker's joined DCL in 1925 Clynelish was absorbed into the expanding DCL empire.

The distillery was silent between 1931 and 1938 and during the war years 1941 to 1945. In the late 1960s a new period of optimism encouraged the owners to build a new concrete and glass distillery

Left: *The gleaming stills that contribute to produce Clynelish, one of the most flavoursome malts in mainland Scotland.*

Above: *The old Clynelish distillery closed when the new distillery was built. Renamed Brora, it re-opened in 1975 but became a casualty of the world recession affecting the whisky industry and it closed permanently in 1983.*

Below: *The new Clynelish was built on a site adjacent to the old distillery and went into production in 1968.*

on an adjacent site slightly uphill from the original site and it was called Clynelish. The original distillery was promptly closed for seven years until another flush of optimism stimulated DCL to rebuild the mash house and re-open it in 1975 as Brora distillery. This delightful old traditional Victorian distillery lived again under its new name for eight years but finally closed its doors in March 1983 during a period of recession in the industry. The stills remain but most of the other distilling equipment has been removed. Brora distillery will not re-open and is now committed to be part of malt whisky history.

The new Clynelish is a six-still distillery built to produce one of the most flavoursome malts outside of Islay. Its connection with Johnnie Walker continues as an important constituent malt used in the Johnnie Walker range of blends. New Clynelish has earned itself a reputation as the producer of a very fine malt and it can confidently look forward to a long future.

1823 MORTLACH (Highland-Speyside)

In 1817 the local laird James Duff, the Earl of Fife, began work on building the new town of Dufftown to provide work for the soldiers returning from the Napoleonic Wars. Six years later, on the wooded banks of the River Dullan, Mortlach was built and it became the first distillery to be licensed in the year of the Excise Act. It had an erratic early career with periods of closure and for a time its barley store became a place of worship during the years that it took to build the new Free Church of Scotland. It was also used as a brewery but in 1851 John Gordon took over and whisky was again produced and sold as 'The Real John Gordon'. He took George Cowie into partnership who succeeded him on his death in 1867. In turn when Cowie died in 1896, his son, Dr Alexander Mitchell Cowie, took over. A year later as the whisky boom was in full swing a new still house was built with six stills and the distillery was connected to the Great North of Scotland Railway. Further expansion took place in 1903 and by 1923, when Cowie sold out to John Walker & Sons, Mortlach was the largest distillery in the area. Two years later the company became part of DCL.

There were further major redevelopments of the distillery in the early 1960s and again in 1996. It is now almost fully mechanised, needing only one man to run the plant. In the hundred years or so since the number of stills was increased to six in 1897 they have always been used individually, and not as is the usual practice in pairs. No two stills are identical and one spirit still, known as the 'Wee Witchie', only produces spirit every third charge. The result

Mortlach's 'Wee Witchie' spirit still is now part of Scotch whisky's own folklore.

of this is that Mortlach's spirit is distilled two-and-a-half times. Mortlach has also retained its larch worm tubs to cool and condense the distillate.

Mortlach is regarded by many as one of Speyside's finest and unsung single malts.

1824 MACALLAN (Highland-Speyside)

Before Thomas Telford built a bridge in 1812 across the river Spey, the cattle drovers from the Highlands had long used the Easter Elchies ford at Craigellachie to take their animals south to sell at market and enjoyed en route the whisky produced at the farm distillery on the site of today's Macallan.

Originally known as Elchies, the distillery was first licensed in 1824 to Alexander Reid, and in 1892, after a number of changes of ownership, an Elgin merchant, Roderick Kemp, who having just sold **Talisker** on Skye, bought and rebuilt the distillery and renamed it Macallan-Glenlivet. The distillery remained in family hands until 1968 when it was converted to a public company, which in turn was taken over by Highland Distillers in 1996.

Macallan's success and ability to survive has been based on its reputation as one of the most desirable malts in many blended whiskies. It was however during the 1960s that the company decided to concentrate production and maturation of Macallan for sale almost entirely as a single malt and by 1978 there were sufficient stocks for the

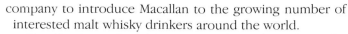

*Above: There are older expressions but the 10-year-old version is the basic model of **The Macallan** which has been referred to as the Rolls Royce amongst malts.*

All casks used at Macallan have previously been used in the sherry industry as can clearly be seen from the stamp of PEDRO DOMECQ of JEREZ on the cask end of this sherry butt.

company to introduce Macallan to the growing number of interested malt whisky drinkers around the world.

Macallan is produced in a very traditional way from the beginning of the process until the moment the whisky is bottled. Golden Promise is the barley used and Macallan uses almost the entire Scottish crop. Most distilleries use either cultured distillers' yeast on its own or mixed with brewers' yeast. Using a cocktail of two distillers' and two brewers' yeasts, the resulting wash from Macallan's fermentation has a strength of around 7.5% abv, slightly lower than that achieved at other distilleries. Macallan has a fine collection of fifteen small stills. They are all of the traditional onion shape and are directly fired using a gas flame with *rummagers* fitted to the wash stills. Most distilleries have an equal number of wash and spirit stills and they are worked in pairs. At Macallan, another point of difference in producing the spirit is the working of their stills in 'trios', one wash still is used with two spirit stills. The lyne arms of Macallan's stills are angled acutely downwards towards the condensers and this contributes to a fuller bodied spirit. The spirit cut in the second distillation is unusual in that only 15% is collected as the *heart of the run*.

Macallan's points of distinction are not yet complete! All Macallan is matured in sherry casks. The timber for the casks is carefully selected in northern Spain from oak trees that are at least eighty years old and the new casks are filled with wine that ferments for several months and then replaced with fino or oloroso sherry wine for a period of two years. This is an expensive process adding to the already high cost of the sherry cask when compared with the American ex-Bourbon cask. After Macallan has been matured for the appropriate number of years, the batch of casks selected for eventual bottling is disgorged at the distillery and filled back into casks for a period of *marrying*. This will be between four and twelve months. It is permissible before bottling whisky to add a small amount of caramel to produce a consistent colour across every bottling. Macallan adds no colouring believing that natural colours and flavours go hand in hand.

Macallan enjoys huge support from the drinkers of malt whisky who can choose from a range starting at the 7-year-old, so enjoyed by the Italians, and then the 10, 12, 18 and 25-year-old expressions.

1824 MILTONDUFF (Highland-Speyside)

Situated on the banks of the Black Burn, a few miles to the south west of Elgin, Miltonduff distillery was built between 1818 and 1824 on the site of a meal mill that had been part of the Benedictine Pluscarden Abbey. Andrew Pearey and Robert Bain were its first owners and it was sold to William Stuart in 1866 who took on Thomas Yool as a partner in 1895. The distillery was extended two years later.

In 1935 Hiram Walker of Canada bought George Ballantine & Son Ltd, the Glasgow firm of wine and Scotch whisky merchants from its owners, James Barclay and R.A. McKinlay. The modest beginning of this company was in 1827 when George Ballantine set up a small grocer's shop in Edinburgh's Cowgate. The business prospered and in 1869 the family established a whisky merchants and exporting business in Glasgow. Ballantine's blended whisky was first available in 1910 and is now the third largest brand in the world with annual sales of four and a half million cases. James Barclay, who stayed with the new company until 1938 and was later to play a key role in the purchase by Seagram of **Strathisla** distillery, was asked to find suitable distilleries to acquire that would produce the quality of malt whisky suitable for the Ballantine's blend. Miltonduff had long been an important malt in the Ballantine's blend and in 1936 Barclay negotiated the purchase of Miltonduff and its near neighbour, **Glenburgie** distillery. This was the point in the history of Scotch whisky that marked the arrival of long-term North American ownership of malt whisky distilleries. In 1987 Miltonduff returned to British ownership when Hiram Walker was bought by Allied Lyons plc. Completely rebuilt in 1975, it is the largest distillery in the Allied group and although most of its whisky is used for blending, a very small quantity is available as a single malt.

In the 1950s and 1960s when different styles of malt whisky were difficult to obtain from competitors, one of the company's technical experts, Alistair Cunningham, designed the *Lomond still*. In the wide neck of the still, there were three rectifying plates that could be placed at different angles to produce varying levels of reflux enabling several different styles of spirit and thus malt whisky to be produced from the same equipment. Lomond stills were installed in several of the company's distilleries to produce a range of malt whisky styles for blending. Inverleven distillery produced Lomond malt whisky, **Glenburgie** produced Glencraig and between 1964 and 1981 Miltonduff produced Mosstowie. The only remaining Lomond still is the wash still installed in Scapa distillery on Orkney. When the distillery was taken out of production in 1993, the Lomond still was not removed and it is

Cardhu is the home of both Johnnie Walker blended whisky and a very successful single malt. The distillery exudes success with its fine modern copper pagoda roofs in sharp contrast to the old whisky warehouses.

used occasionally when the distillery is taken out of mothballs for brief periods to produce a small batch of spirit to maintain the supply of Scapa malt whisky.

1824 CARDHU (Highland-Speyside)

John Cumming was a convicted smuggler and in 1811, on a hillside half a mile from the river Spey, he leased Cardow farm and from the outset, along with his wife Helen, made illicit whisky. He licensed the distillery in 1824 and when he died in 1846 he was succeeded by his son Lewis who continued to work the distillery. Late in life Lewis married Elizabeth Robertson and when he died in 1872 she ran the business to support their young family.

Elizabeth decided that with the strong growth in demand for Cardow's whisky in the 1870s and early 1880s a new distillery was needed. 'New Cardow' was built on land adjacent to the old distillery and in October 1885 the first cask was filled for Robert

Sanderson & Co. of Leith, a customer of forty years standing. Elizabeth was regarded as an accomplished distiller and businesswoman and was known affectionately as 'The Queen of the Whisky Trade'. Stills and other old equipment from the old Cardow distillery were sold in 1886 to William Grant for use in **Glenfiddich**, the distillery he was building at Dufftown. In 1893 Elizabeth sold Cardow to one of her largest customers, John Walker & Sons Ltd of Kilmarnock. As part of the deal her son John, who had been running Cardow for a few years, was appointed a director of Walkers. The company went public in 1923 and became part of DCL two years later.

The distillery was rebuilt and expanded to six stills in 1960 and most of its production was destined to support the blend of Johnnie Walker's Red and Black blended whiskies. Cardow's whisky was always known as Cardhu and in 1982 the distillery became officially known as Cardhu. This coincided with the wide availability of Cardhu single malt whisky, packaged in a distinctive pinched square bottle, and strongly promoted in many markets around the world. It is a very successful brand with sales of a quarter of a million cases making it the third largest brand after Glenfiddich and Glenmorangie.

Cardhu is a story of sustained success. It has readily survived through good business sense and the closest association with the world's most successful blended whisky.

Johnnie Walker

In 1820 John Walker established his grocer's business in the Ayrshire town of Kilmarnock and the first steps in creating the Walker whisky empire were taken in the middle of the nineteenth century when the family began to sell on a wholesaling basis their own 'Walker's Kilmarnock blended whiskies'. On the death of John Walker in 1857, his son Alexander succeeded him. With the change in the law to allow the blending of malt and grain whiskies under bond, Alexander developed a flourishing business in blended whisky, registering in 1867 the copyright to Walker's Old Highland Whisky. By the late 1870s, Walker's whisky was being sold in the distinctive square bottle that is still in use today. A sales office was opened in London in 1880 and one in Australia ten years later. The family firm became a private limited company in 1886 and within two years they were exporting to over seventy countries. The next logical move was to buy Cardhu distillery in 1893 and thus guarantee the supply of its high-quality Speyside malt whisky to support the rapidly growing sales of the company's blends.

In 1906 the company's oldest blend, the 12-year-old Extra Special Old Highland Whisky, was made distinguishable from the

Above: *Another example of Johnnie Walker's wartime advertising, this time in a 1940 issue of* The London Illustrated News, *where good whisky went hand-in-hand with the patriotic work of digging for victory.*

Opposite: *With the war over, Johnnie Walker strides forward in confident mood in Clive Uptton's advertising illustration of 1951.*

TIME MARCHES ON!

JOHNNIE WALKER
SCOTCH WHISKY
Born 1820 —
still going
strong

It makes me proud to think I've seen
The paddle-boat become the "Queen."
Like Clyde-built ships, I've grown in fame —
The skill behind me's still the same.

Special Old Highland Whisky by using a black rather than a red label.

'Johnnie Walker' was registered as a trademark in 1908 and a year later the first advertisement appeared using cartoonist Tom Browne's interpretation of a strutting, monocled 'Johnnie Walker – Born 1820 – Still Going Strong'.

In 1932 Johnnie Walker Swing was introduced with an eye on the North American market.

The Special Red Label and the Extra Special Black Label versions were both packaged in the unique square bottle. Growth of both brands has been remarkable with Red Label firmly established for years as the largest selling blend in the world with sales of nearly eight million cases and the de-luxe Black Label enjoys sales of three-and-a-half million cases. In order to protect export sales of Red Label into Europe, without precedent, it was decided in 1977 to withdraw the brand from sale in Britain. It was a difficult and painful decision because in the six years it was not available the supermarket groups developed their own label brands and both Bell's and The Famous Grouse became increasingly popular premium-priced brands. The much changed market left little room for Johnnie Walker's return and its sales in the UK are very small.

In addition to Johnnie Walker Red Label, Black Label and Swing, the Gold, Blue and Pure Malt versions have been introduced in recent years.

1824 BALMENACH (Highland-Speyside)

James McGregor, believed to be an experienced illicit distiller from Tomintoul, established himself as the licensed distiller on Balmenach farm in 1824. Magnificently situated in the Haughs (Hills) of Cromdale, a few miles east of Grantown-on-Spey, the area had fine local peat and plentiful supplies of water from the springs that flowed from the Cromdale Hills.

Barnard noted in his visit of 1887 that 'like all other parts of the establishment, the building and its contents are of the most antiquated type.' In 1897, considerable improvements were made

Balmenach as recorded on a postcard of around 1910.

to the distillery and a private branch railway line, which was to be used for seventy years, was built to link the distillery with Cromdale station, a mile-and-a-half away.

After almost one hundred years of ownership in the McGregor family, the distillery was sold to a consortium of three whisky blending companies in 1922 and three years later these companies and Balmenach were acquired by DCL. Used by the army during the Second World War, the distillery was expanded to six stills in 1962 and in 1964 the floor maltings were replaced by Saladin maltings until they were made redundant in the mid 1980s. Closed in 1993, the distillery was bought by Inver House Distillers in 1997 and brought back into production in March 1998. Balmenach is a little unusual in having 'worms' in a cast iron tub of 1928 vintage to condense the distillate.

1824 FETTERCAIRN (Highland)

Fettercairn distillery was converted from a cornmill by Sir James Ramsay and in 1824 was leased to its first tenant, James Stewart. In its first sixty years the distillery had several changes of ownership.

Badly damaged by fire in 1887 the distillery was rebuilt and reopened three years later as The Fettercairn Distillery Co., with Sir John Gladstone, father of Prime Minister William Gladstone, as its chairman. The distillery changed hands again in 1923 and ceased production three years later. It was near to being dismantled, when in 1939 Train & MacIntyre, a Glasgow firm of wine and spirit merchants, through its subsidiary Associated Scottish Distilleries, acquired the distillery. This company was part of National Distillers of America and had already bought six distilleries including **Bruichladdich** and **Benromach**. The Americans sold the company to DCL in 1954, but Fettercairn was not part of the deal it being sold separately to an Aberdeen businessman, Tom Scott Sutherland. The distillery was enlarged in the 1960s and a second pair of stills was installed. In 1971 Fettercairn was sold yet again, this time to the **Tomintoul**-Glenlivet

With the closure in the last twenty years of four distilleries in Stonehaven, Montrose and Brechin, Fettercairn is the sole survivor in this beautiful farming area of Angus, some twenty-five miles south-west of Aberdeen.

Co. and following a succession of owners of that company, Fettercairn is now owned by Whyte & Mackay.

Surviving in spite of its pre-war closure and its many changes of ownership, Fettercairn has a good traditional feel to it and steadily produces whisky for blending and for sale as a single malt, Fettercairn 1824.

1824 THE GLENLIVET (Highland-Speyside)

The Glen of the river Livet was a wild and rough area in the early nineteenth century and it was home to many illicit distillers and smugglers. One of their number, George Smith, was the first successful applicant to become a legal operator of a distillery in Glenlivet and he set up business at Upper Drumin farm in 1824 and his first whisky began to flow early the following year. As with many small distillers at the time he soon experienced cash flow problems and if it had not been for the help of his landlord, the Duke of Gordon, owner of the Glenlivet estate, George Smith

would have gone out of business. His whisky found a ready market in the populous areas of Scotland and in 1853 one of his agents, the enterprising Andrew Usher in Leith, developed a blend of malts, 'Old Vatted Glenlivet', which gained great popularity both in Britain and in overseas markets.

Such was the demand for The Glenlivet that in 1859 George Smith built a new distillery at Minmore, a few hundred yards from Drumin. By the time of his death in 1871, when his son John Gordon Smith succeeded him, The Glenlivet was firmly established as the most successful whisky in London. J.G. Smith was concerned that other distilleries were incorporating 'Glenlivet' in the name of their distilleries and their whiskies. After a great deal of legal action it was eventually ruled that Smith's Glenlivet distillery was only one entitled to be called *The* Glenlivet and that a further ten distilleries were allowed to use Glenlivet but only as a suffix to the distillery name.

In 1901 J.G. Smith died and, having not married, the business passed to his nephew, George Smith Grant. The business remained in the hands of the Grant family until 1952 when G. & J.G. Grant merged with **Glen Grant** to form The Glenlivet & Glen Grant Distilleries Ltd. A further merger in 1970 with **Longmorn-Glenlivet** Distillers and the bottlers Hill Thomson, produced The Glenlivet Distillers Ltd and six years later this enlarged group was acquired by the Canadian giant drinks company, Seagram. Following the sale by Seagram of their whisky interests in 2001, The Glenlivet is now part of Pernod Ricard.

The Glenlivet is a large distillery boasting eight impressive stills. The fragrant medium-bodied malt with a hint of fruit, some sweetness and a touch of sherry is a great favourite in the United States and was described by Neil Gunn nearly seventy years ago 'as a synonym for the real stuff'.

1825 LINKWOOD (Highland-Speyside)

Peter Brown, the factor of the Seafield estates and recognised as one of the foremost nineteenth-century agricultural improvers in the rich agricultural area a few miles to the south of Elgin, built Linkwood distillery in 1825 and it remained in family hands until 1897. Floated in that year as Linkwood-Glenlivet Distillery Ltd, Innes Cameron, a whisky broker from Elgin, joined the board in 1902 and became its Managing Director and main shareholder. Shortly after his death in 1932 DCL's subsidiary SMD acquired the company.

When the distillery reopened after its closure for four years during the Second World War, Roderick MacKenzie a Gaelic-speaking native of Wester Ross was appointed distillery manager.

The Glenlivet 12-year-old single malt.

During his eighteen-year tenure of that job he insisted that cobwebs in the distillery were not to be removed for fear of changing the character of the whisky!

As with others in the DCL group, Linkwood was treated to an extensive rebuilding in the early 1960s and in 1971 a second distillery was built with a mash tun, five wash backs and four stills. The mashing is carried out in the 'new' distillery and some of the wort is piped to the 'old' to be fermented in the six wash backs there. Most of the wash is distilled in the 'new' although the two stills in the 'old' are occasionally used and these retain their traditional worms in a splendid rectangular cast iron tank.

Linkwood distillery has had a long and uneventful career and is an attractive blend of new and old. It steadily produces high-quality Speyside malt whisky suited to the blending requirements of Diageo, the owner of so many big brands.

1825 AUCHENTOSHAN (Lowland)

Auchentoshan, **Bladnoch** and **Glenkinchie** are the three Lowland distilleries to survive into the twenty-first century. Located to the west of Glasgow on the north side of the River Clyde, this old and attractive distillery is increasingly being surrounded by encroaching housing estates. It is located very close to the line that demarcates Highland from Lowland and confounds some experts by drawing its water supply for whisky making from the Old Kilpatrick Hills which are clearly in the Highland area! The distillery has had many owners in its long life and along with Banff distillery, which was closed in 1983, has the rare and unfortunate distinction of having suffered considerable bomb damage during the last war. Largely rebuilt after the war, Auchentoshan was bought by the Scottish brewers J. & R. Tennent Ltd in the early 1960s and in 1974 they sold it to Eadie Cairns, Glasgow-based blenders, wholesalers and retailers. Ten years later, Stanley P. Morrison, who had already acquired **Bowmore** and **Glen Garioch** distilleries, became Auchentoshan's new owner. In 1995, Stanley P. Morrison became part of the Japanese drinks group, Suntory.

This is Scotland's only distillery to use one wash, one intermediate and one spirit still to triple distil the spirit to a final high strength of 82% abv, which when matured for at least ten years in ex-Bourbon casks produces a delicately fragrant, smooth and light malt. Auchentoshan, made from unpeated malt and with water containing little trace of any peat, is marketed as *Glasgow's* malt and increasingly, its older expressions, the 21, 25 and the rare 31-year-old versions stand out as being of exceptional interest.

The wash and intermediate stills used in Auchentoshan's triple distillation are of the same tall and elegant lantern design as this, the spirit still.

1825 BEN NEVIS (Highland)

John Macdonald, who built the distillery at the foot of Ben Nevis, Britain's highest mountain, was a very tall man and his nickname, Long John, was to become a household name for whisky during the twentieth century. Following his death in 1865, his son Donald P. Macdonald took over the distillery and rapidly developed the pure Highland malt whisky, 'Long John's Celebrated Dew of Ben Nevis'. The demand was so great that he built the Nevis distillery nearby which operated between 1878 and 1908. Ben Nevis distillery remained in the hands of the Macdonald family until they sold it to Joseph Hobbs in 1955. Hobbs had previous experience in the whisky industry in the late 1930s when, acting on behalf of the National Distilleries of America, he was instrumental in buying through their Glasgow-based subsidiary, Train & McIntyre, a clutch of distilleries, most of which were sold to DCL in 1954. He introduced some interesting practices into Ben Nevis. Firstly he built a small Coffey patent still and installed two wash backs constructed in concrete. Each wash back was subdivided into four thus making a total of eight concrete fermenting vessels. He was also known to use beer barrels to mature whisky and another 'first' was what he called

Left: The mass of Ben Nevis, Britain's highest mountain, provides a fine background to the distillery that shares its name.

Right: A very rare example of Long John's 'Celebrated Dew of Ben Nevis' believed to have been bottled in 1882.

'blending at birth'. This was the blending of new spirit from his pot stills with new grain spirit from his patent still and then filled into casks for the period of maturation.

Distilling at Ben Nevis was discontinued in 1978 and Long John International, a subsidiary of the English brewing company Whitbread, bought the distillery in 1981. This was an interesting coincidence because the registered brand name, Long John, was transferred in 1921 to W.H. Chaplin, a wine and spirit merchant with offices in Glasgow and London. Seager Evans, a long-established London firm of distillers and wine and spirit merchants, bought Chaplin's in 1936 and in turn were taken over by an American company, Schenley Industries Inc. in 1956. In 1975, Whitbread bought Schenley's subsidiary, Long John International, and brought the brand, Long John, back into British ownership. Ben Nevis was reopened for a brief spell of production in the mid-1980s but closed again in 1986. The distillery was sold to the Nikka Whisky Distillery Co. of Japan in 1989 and they reopened it in the following year. The last ten years has provided the distillery with a good period of stability and the opportunity to develop a consistent supply of stock for both the blending market, including the distillery's own 'Dew of Ben Nevis', and a small quantity of Ben Nevis, the single malt.

1825 EDRADOUR (Highland)

Beautifully situated straddling a rushing burn in the heart of the finest Perthshire countryside, Edradour survives as the last example of the once numerous Perthshire farm-distilleries. It is the smallest of all Scotland's distilleries and has within it some unique distilling equipment. It is believed that a group of local farmers began distilling in 1825 in the buildings that survive to this day and they called their distillery Glenforres.

The distillery's name had been changed to Edradour by the time Barnard paid his visit in 1886:

> The distillery, which was built in 1837, is situated at the foot of a steep hill on the road side, and consists of a few ancient buildings not unlike a farmstead, past which flows one of the most rampant and brawling streams in the district. On either side of this river, heather in rich abundance hangs from the banks and jutting corners of the rocks, and there is water power sufficient to drive several water-wheels.

Descendants of one of that founding group of farmers, William McIntosh, ran the distillery until 1925 when William Whiteley, a blender from Glasgow and Leith, bought the distillery to guarantee the supply of malt whisky in his House of Lords and King's Ransom blends.

During the period of Prohibition in the United States, Whiteley is reputed to have supplied whisky to smugglers in specially toughened square bottles capable of withstanding rough treatment, including being fired on to beaches in torpedoes!

Campbell Distillers, part of the French drinks group Pernod Ricard, bought the distillery in 1983 and three years later Edradour became available as a single malt with current annual production of three thousand cases.

In July 2002 the distillery was sold to the Edinburgh based Signatory Vintage Scotch Whisky Company.

Everything about the distillery is small. The malting of the barley was discontinued in 1938 and very lightly peated ready-milled malt (grist) is brought in sacks direct from the maltster.

Above: *Edradour as it looked seventy years ago and as it looks today. This is a classic example of a farm distillery.*

Right: *To cool the worts prior to fermentation Edradour uses the only surviving Morton refrigerator.*

The cast iron mash tun is believed to be at least one hundred years old and is unusual in being one of the few remaining in the industry open at the top and complete with a traditional raking system. The wort is then cooled in a Morton refrigerator, the only one to survive in the industry, before being transferred to ferment in one of the two Oregon pine wash backs. The spirit that flows from each of Edradour's two very small stills is condensed through worms set in tanks of cold running water immediately behind the still house. The spirit is aged exclusively in oloroso sherry casks to produce a light 10-year-old malt whisky, slightly sweet with a taste of honeyed fruit.

1826 PULTENEY (Highland)

Wick is one of the most northerly towns in Scotland and for many years was a major fishing port. In the early nineteenth century the British Fisheries Society under its first chairman, Sir William Pulteney MP, commissioned the engineer Thomas Telford to build a new harbour and a fishing village for 1,500 people on the south side of the River Wick opposite the existing town. The village was called Pulteneytown and by the middle of the century had become the largest herring port in Europe. In May 1922 Wick, having experienced years of lawlessness as the result of drunkenness among the large working population, imposed a period of Prohibition which was to last for exactly twenty-five years!

In 1826 an experienced distiller, James Henderson, built a distillery in the new village of Pulteneytown. This, the most northerly distillery on mainland Scotland, is of a traditional courtyard layout built in distinctive Caithness stone and is one of a handful of distilleries to have been built in an urban setting.

The distillery remained in the family's hands until 1920 when it was bought by James Watson & Sons Ltd of Dundee who were taken over by John Dewar in 1923 and then became part of DCL in 1925. Closed in 1926, Pulteney risked permanent closure until brought back to life in 1951 by the owner of **Balblair**, Robert Cumming. Four years later Cumming retired and sold the distillery to Hiram Walker, who by then were owners of four other malt whisky distilleries – **Miltonduff, Glenburgie, Scapa** and Glencadam. In 1995, ten years after Allied Distillers had acquired Hiram Walker, Pulteney was sold to Inver House Distillers.

The distillery is small with just one pair of stills. The wash still is of an unusual shape with a large boil pot and a short truncated neck. This still was originally bought from a distillery in Campbeltown about a hundred years ago and being too tall to be installed in the

still house the rounded top of the swan neck was cut off. The spirit still has a purifier installed on the lyne arm to assist the making of a lighter spirit. The spirit is condensed through traditional worm tubs in water brought to the distillery from Loch Hempriggs along a three-mile lade built by Thomas Telford.

In 1997 Pulteney's new owners introduced the Old Pulteney 12-year-old single malt whisky which in its packaging strongly associates itself with Wick's long but now defunct history of herring fishing. With a deep amber colour, Old Pulteney is smooth, medium bodied dry with a hint of saltiness. The whisky from Pulteney has for some time been known as the 'Manzanilla of malt whiskies'.

Left: There are stills with intriguing designs at Dalmore, Glenmorangie and Glen Grant but Pulteney's wash still is bafflingly grotesque with its very large boil pot and short truncated neck!

Below: The close link between the herring industry, Wick and Pulteney is fully expressed in the packaging of Pulteney 12-year-old.

Glendronach's maltings and old kiln were last used prior to the distillery being mothballed in 1996. The distillery re-opened in 2002 but malted barley is now being brought in to the distillery.

1826 GLENDRONACH (Highland)

A few miles to the northeast of Huntly in Aberdeenshire, the distillery was built in 1826 by a consortium of farmers and businessmen led by James Allardes. Badly damaged by fire in 1837, the distillery was bought by Walter Scott in 1852. In 1920 Captain Charles Grant, son of

Curling and whisky have long had a close association. 1920s advertising for Teacher's Highland Cream illustrated by Cecil Aldin.

William Grant of **Glenfiddich**, bought Glendronach. The distillery was in Grant's ownership until sold in 1960 to William Teacher & Sons Ltd. The distillery was mothballed in 1996. It reopened in 2002 and it is the only distillery to retain its coal-fired stills. Available as a single malt, Glendronach along with **Ardmore** is a fingerprint malt in the blend of Teacher's Highland Cream.

1828 SPRINGBANK (Campbeltown)

The earliest known licensed distillery in Campbeltown was called Campbeltown and was established in 1815 or 1817. Twenty years after the 1823 Excise Act there were thirty licensed distilleries in the town. By the time of Barnard's visit to 'The Whisky City' in 1887, there were twenty-one distilleries employing 250 people and producing nearly two million gallons of whisky.

It is possible that the craft of whisky making in Scotland was first brought over to Kintyre from Antrim in Northern Ireland. Kintyre had plenty of peat, water and barley and was a natural place for illicit distillation. The only coal mine in the western Highlands, Drumlemble colliery near Machrihanish, was an additional factor in the development of commercial whisky making in the area. A short canal was built to carry the coal by barge to Campbeltown and this

At Springbank there is little sign of the modern look. If it is not broken, there has been no need to replace it.

was replaced in the 1870s by means of a narrow-gauge railway.

The demand for whisky by the blenders in Scotland's central belt was growing rapidly in the 1880s and 1890s. The quality of Campbeltown's whiskies however was compromised as the distillers tried to keep supplies in line with the increased demand. They cut corners by speeding up the process of distillation, cutting back on the period of maturation and using cheap and second-rate casks. Campbeltown whiskies were inferior to the new range of whiskies produced on Speyside and the blenders turned away from the firewater of Campbeltown. In the early 1920s Hazelburn, the biggest and oldest distillery, tried to distance itself from other Campbeltown distilleries by calling itself a 'Kintyre' whisky. Springbank and Glen Nevis preferred to be known as 'West Highland'. A number of the distillers sought to supply bootleg whisky to the United States during the period of Prohibition. This did little to put off the eventual demise of the Campbeltown distilling business. The area's remoteness from the blending area in the central belt, the exhaustion by 1923 of supplies from the local coal mine and the blenders' dislike of Campbeltown's 'stinking fish' whiskies saw most of the distilleries going out of business during the years 1922 to 1928. Riechlachan distillery survived until 1936 and **Glen Scotia** and **Springbank** survive as today's representatives of the once great days of Campbeltown's whisky making.

The Reid family established Springbank in 1828 and following financial difficulties the Mitchells took over the business in 1837.

The spirit safe at Springbank distillery is believed to be the oldest in Scotland.

It is no surprise that Springbank's unique wash still is one of the few remaining examples in the whisky industry of a still with sections secured with rivets.

The distillery is to this day licensed to J.&A. Mitchell and Co. Ltd and it is the oldest continuously family-owned distillery in Scotland.

Springbank closed for three years in the 1920s and again in the recession in the 1980s.

It is a distillery that has maintained more of the traditional ways of making whisky than any other in Scotland. Springbank is unique in completing all aspects of whisky making from malting its entire barley requirement through to the maturation and bottling of its range of malt and blended whiskies. There are two malting seasons in the year and the four distillery workers steep the barley, germinate it on the malting floors and dry it in the kiln. When sufficient malt has been made, the four men then turn their skills to operate the hundred-year-old cast iron mash tun, ferment the wort in the six boatskin larch wash backs and make the spirit in the three stills.

The wash still is unique, heated by a live flame and complete with a rummager. The two spirit stills differ in that the first has a worm condenser and the second has a conventional condenser. Springbank is not triple distilled but it is more correctly distilled two and a half times. The low wines at a strength of 25% abv are distilled in the first spirit still to produce feints at between 50% and 55% abv. Of these feints, 80% are put into the second spirit still with 20% of low wines and the spirit that is kept from this distillation is at a strength of 72% abv. The foreshots and feints are added back into the first spirit still with the next batch of low wines.

The spirit is matured in both sherry and ex-Bourbon casks and the whisky is manually filtered rather than chill-filtered prior to bottling. Chill filtering has become common practice in the industry since the 1970s. The temperature of the whisky is lowered to near freezing point to encourage the microscopic particles, which can cause a haze to the final whisky when water and ice is added, to become suspended and more easily removed during filtration. These particles are loaded however with flavoursome characteristics and are kept rather than discarded at Springbank. The whiskies are bottled on site in a bottling hall that used to be one of the warehouses of the neighbouring Longrow distillery.

A second malt whisky occasionally made in the Springbank distillery is **Longrow**. It is distilled conventionally in two stills using malt which is entirely peat kilned for fifty hours, giving it a heavy almost Islay quality. There is also a third malt whisky in the making at Springbank, **Hazelburn**. Unpeated, the barley is kilned using hot air only for thirty hours. The wash is distilled to make the low wines and then distilled in the first of the

spirit stills to produce the feints. These are then distilled in the second spirit still to produce a high strength spirit which has undergone a genuine triple distillation. The first spirit to be matured as Hazelburn was distilled in 1997 and it is not expected to be available until it is at least ten years old.

1830 TALISKER (Island)

In 1825 brothers Hugh and Kenneth MacAskill moved to Skye from the small Hebridean island of Eigg firstly to farm sheep and then in 1830, on land leased from the Macleod family, they built Talisker distillery in the coastal hamlet of Carbost at the head of Loch Harport. After a succession of owners, Alexander Grigor Allan and Roderick Kemp acquired the distillery in 1880 and rebuilt it. Kemp sold his interest in 1892 and bought **Macallan** distillery. After merging with **Dailuaine** in 1898, Talisker was enlarged and two years later a pier was built connected to the distillery by a short length of tramway to facilitate the loading of casks on to the small coastal ships known locally as puffers. Thomas Mackenzie became a major shareholder and managing director and a year after his death in 1915 a consortium of owners including John Dewar & Sons Ltd and John Walker & Sons Ltd took control of the company and in 1925 all was absorbed into DCL.

After the distillery was badly damaged by fire in 1960, the still house was rebuilt and five replacement stills were installed, identical to those destroyed in the fire. Talisker and **Macduff** are the only two distilleries in Scotland to have the unusual combination of two wash and three spirit stills and until 1928 Talisker's spirit was triple distilled. Both wash stills have lyne arms with an unusual 'U' shape to encourage extra reflux and thus purer low wines are then worked by the spirit stills. Talisker boasts the traditional worm form of condenser each in its wooden tub situated outside the still house.

There have been few legal distilleries on Skye. Three opened in the early 1800s but none of them survived for more than two years. In spite of poor management in its first fifty years, Talisker established a good reputation for the quality of its whisky. The arrival of John Walker and then DCL in the early twentieth century secured the future of Talisker. This distinctive island malt whisky became an important constituent in the Johnnie Walker blends and the Johnnie Walker logo was incorporated within the Talisker label until the 1980s.

Johnnie Walker's strong association with Talisker was incorporated into the label design of Talisker's 12-year-old single malt until the early 1980s.

Talisker 10-year-old single malt became one of the range of six Classic Malts in 1989 and is marketed at the unusually high strength of 45.8% abv.

1833 GLENGOYNE (Highland)

Fifteen miles north of Glasgow, Glengoyne distillery is attractively sited in a wooded glen at the foot of Dumgoyne Hill. It is the most southerly of the Highland distilleries and is actually sited on the Highland/Lowland line. Its water supply is from north of the line and the warehouses where the whisky is matured are just to the south of the line!

Archibald McLellan established Glenguin distillery in 1833. At a later date the distillery was renamed Burnfoot of Dumgoyne and when Lang Brothers, a Glasgow firm of whisky merchants and

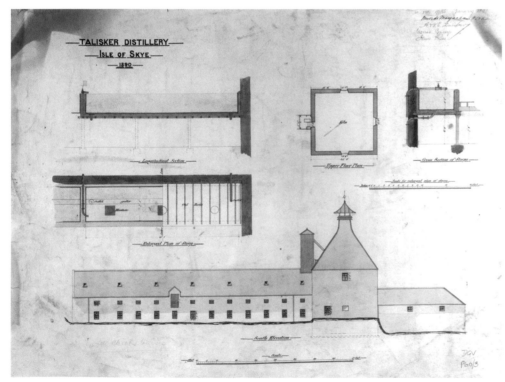

Top: *A 1911 postcard of Talisker distillery in the hamlet of Carbost.*

Above: *Detail from the plans of 1890 to build additional maltings and kiln at Talisker.*

Right: *Detail from a late nineteenth-century painting of Glengoyne distillery.*

blenders, bought it in 1877 they changed the name to Glengoyne. Lang Brothers merged with the Robertson and Baxter Group in 1964 and Glengoyne distillery was sold in 2003 to the independent blending and bottling company, Ian MacLeod & Co. Ltd.

When the distillery was rebuilt in 1967 a third still was added and the spirit produced from the large wash still is sufficient to charge both spirit stills. Unlike most distilleries that malted their own requirements until the 1960s, Glengoyne has used a commercial supplier of malted barley since 1910. It uses a totally unpeated malt and its water supply, the Distillery Burn flowing from Dumboyne Hill, is also devoid of any peat content. Distillation is at one of the slowest rates in the industry and the whisky produced is quite characteristically a Lowland malt, totally lacking any peat influence, pale in colour, fresh and light in taste.

1835 GLEN SCOTIA (Campbeltown)

Starting life as Scotia, this small unexceptional distillery with its two stills is a surprising survivor of the days when Campbeltown was 'The Whisky City' with more than a score of distilleries. Whilst **Springbank** has had a successful career under the control of its founding family, Glen Scotia has had many changes of ownership and several periods of closure. The distillery has been out of production for twelve of the last twenty years. Now under the same ownership as **Loch Lomond** distillery, there is hope for the survival of Glen Scotia. When **Springbank** is silent its distilling team transfers to Glen Scotia and makes small quantities of a traditional, quite heavily-peated spirit from its two stills. There is both optimism and enthusiasm that this style of Glen Scotia will help the distillery emerge securely from its difficult and uncertain past.

1835 BENRINNES (Highland-Speyside)

The granite mountain of Ben Rinnes rises to a height of 840 metres and provides the water supply to a dozen distilleries in its vicinity. Benrinnes distillery was founded on its present site in 1835, replacing another of the same name built ten years earlier at nearby Whitehouse Farm that was destroyed and swept away in the great Speyside floods of 1829.

Barnard commented during his visit in 1887 that 'its water rises from springs on the summit of the mountain and can be seen on a clear day some miles distant, sparkling over the prominent rocks on its downward course, passing over mossy banks and gravel,

Glen Scotia distillery.

Rebuilt in the 1950s and 1960s, Benrinnes may have lost its connection with its Victorian origin and design but not its close association with the mountain after which it is named.

which perfectly filters it.' The owner at the time of Barnard's visit was David Edward and on his death was succeeded by his son, Alexander, who built **Craigellachie** and **Aultmore** distilleries. Benrinnes was largely rebuilt after a fire in 1896 and three large stills were installed. The distillery suffered badly from the Pattison crash in 1898 and John Dewar & Sons Ltd took control of the company in 1922 and they in turn became part of DCL in 1925.

The distillery was reconstructed in 1955 and ten years later three additional stills were installed. Benrinnes produces spirit by means of a form of triple distillation and the make comes off the stills at 75.5% abv. The distillery is one of the sixteen distilleries to use traditional worms to cool the distillate.

Not open to the public visitor, Benrinnes is one of twenty-seven distilleries owned by Diageo and it produces high-quality malt whisky for use in the large portfolio of blends owned by the company.

1836 GLENFARCLAS
(Highland-Speyside)

Glenfarclas was first licensed in 1836 to Robert Hay, the tenant farmer of Rechlerich Farm that is situated on the western side of Ben Rinnes. Hay died in 1865 and the vacant farm attracted the prominent local Grant family. The Grants became tenants of the farm and bought the distillery equipment for £519 19s 0d (£519.95). Their prime interest was in farming and breeding cattle so they leased the distillery to John Smith for four years until 1869 when he left to build **Cragganmore** distillery. The Grant family then took over the running of the distillery until 1895 when they formed the Glenfarclas-Glenlivet Distillery Co. in which they held an equal interest with the blending company, Pattison & Co. of Leith. The distillery was rebuilt in 1897 and its output was doubled. The 'Pattison's Crash' in 1898 put the future of the distillery in jeopardy.

The brothers John and George reformed the family partnership of J. & G. Grant, sold their entire stock of whisky and with large bank loans managed to meet the company's debts. The company steadily rebuilt its prosperity in the 1920s and 1930s and Glenfarclas distillery is now in the hands of the fifth generation of the Grant family.

Bottled at its cask strength of 60% pure alcohol, Glenfarclas 105 derives its name from the pre-1980 Sikes system of calculating the strength of spirits where pure alcohol was 175 degrees proof. (60% of 175 = 105).

After 135 years of family control, Glenfarclas is an outstanding example of a truly independent family controlled business that has successfully survived the ravages of time.

It is a distillery with some interesting equipment. The mash tun is the largest in the industry, with a ten-metre diameter and taking a sixteen-and-a-half tonne mash. The stills are the largest of any Speyside distillery, unusual in being heated by external gas flame and each of the wash stills is fitted with a rummager.

There is a lot of warehousing space at Glenfarclas with a capacity for the storage of over 85,000 casks. Most of Glenfarclas is matured in sherry butts or plain oak casks. The use of ex-Bourbon casks is eschewed. Glenfarclas was the pioneer of cask strength whiskies and Glenfarclas 105 bottled at 60% abv is a classic in its own right.

The visitor centre was opened in 1973 and welcomes around 80,000 visitors in a year. It has an oak-panelled reception area, unusual in having been constructed with timber from the passenger liner SS *Tirpitz*, which was built in Germany in 1913 and renamed the SS *Empress of Australia* when bought by Canadian Pacific.

1837 GLENKINCHIE (Lowland)

Less than twenty miles to the east of Edinburgh is an area of countryside described by Robert Burns as 'the most glorious corn country as I have ever seen'. Moss and Hume in their definitive book, *The Making of Scotch Whisky*, recorded that over 210 licensed distilleries were established in the Lowland area between the middle of the eighteenth century and the end of the nineteenth. Many of these distilleries had very brief lives. In 1825, when over a hundred distilleries were operating in the Lowland area, two farming brothers, John and George Rate, began making whisky in a distillery known as Milton. In 1837 they re-named the distillery Glenkinchie after the Kinchie burn that supplied it. Today, only three of those Lowland distilleries survive; **Auchentoshan** near Glasgow, **Bladnoch** near Wigton and Glenkinchie.

In 1853 the brothers went bankrupt and the distillery fell into disuse with part of it being used as a sawmill. In 1881 a group of whisky blenders, wine merchants and brewers from Edinburgh,

The detailed models of worm tubs, two lantern stills and a mash tun in Glenkinchie's remarkable Museum of Malt Whisky Production.

enthused by the rapidly developing whisky business, brought the distillery back to life. Incorporated in 1890 as Glenkinchie Distillery Co. Ltd the distillery was rebuilt in red brick and fully re-equipped.

In 1914, in a move to protect the interests of the Lowland malt whisky distillers, Glenkinchie joined forces with four other distillery companies (Rosebank, St Magdalene, Grange and Clydesdale) to form Scottish Malt Distillers. Eleven years later in 1925, SMD amalgamated with DCL.

Glenkinchie distillery has been regularly improved over the years but retains traditional Oregon pine and Canadian larch wash backs, two stills almost bloated in their enormity and worms in a large cast-iron tank used to cool the spirit. The stills have thick swan necks and lyne arms that are angled sharply downwards.

Glenkinchie 10-year-old was selected as the Lowland malt in the Classic Malt range. The water used in the distillation is from the Lammermuir Hills and is unusually hard, having picked up calcium whilst running over limestone in the hills. Pale golden in colour, Glenkinchie is sweetly dry, light, fresh and spicy. Its makers suggest that the whisky is ideal as an aperitif, a whisky for refined tastes. This is obviously why they call it 'The Edinburgh Malt'!

The old red-brick building that housed the floor maltings until they were closed in 1968 has proved to be an ideal home for the Museum of Malt Whisky Production. This was the idea of Alistair Munro, manager of the distillery at that time who, realising how fast the distilling industry was changing, felt that the disappearing past should be preserved and recorded for the future. The largest item in the museum is a model of a malt whisky distillery. It was built to the impressively large scale of one-sixth of actual size by Basset-Lowke of Northampton for use as part of the Scotch Whisky exhibit displayed in the Palace of Industry at the British Empire Exhibition held at Wembley in 1924-1925. The model was then lent to the Science Museum in London until 1948 when it was put into storage until its eventual return to DCL in 1963. The model is in splendid condition and shows most clearly the process from malting to maturation. In the many distilleries that open their doors to visitors there are many fascinating pieces of old equipment, artifacts, photographs and other records of the history of the whisky industry. Glenkinchie's model distillery, probably because of its size and detail, its splendid condition and the fact that it over seventy-five years old, is without doubt the most remarkable surviving reminder of the past history of the whisky industry!

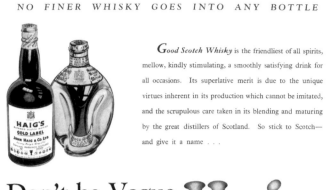

NO FINER WHISKY GOES INTO ANY BOTTLE

Good Scotch Whisky is the friendliest of all spirits, mellow, kindly stimulating, a smoothly satisfying drink for all occasions. Its superlative merit is due to the unique virtues inherent in its production which cannot be imitated, and the scrupulous care taken in its blending and maturing by the great distillers of Scotland. So stick to Scotch— and give it a name . . .

Don't be Vague ask for Haig

Above: *Advertising in the early 1950s of Haig's Gold Label in its dumpy bottle alongside the unique Haig Dimple.*

Right: *Haig Dimple as the Americans know it: Pinch, with the somewhat extravagant claim made in the 1950s – 'A pleasure that has grown steadily for over three centuries . . . to receive a bottle of Pinch'!*

Glenkinchie has for many years been licensed to John Haig & Co. Ltd of Markinch in Fife and has been an important malt in the renowned blends of that company.

Haig Gold Label

John Haig established a grain distillery in Cameron Bridge in Fife and by the 1850s was producing blended whiskies. In the 1870s the blended side of the business was transferred to nearby Markinch. John Haig and Co. merged with DCL in 1919. Haig's whiskies sold well both at home and overseas and by 1939, at the outbreak of the Second World War, Haig Gold Label blended Scotch whisky had become the largest selling brand in Britain. After the war Haig, in its familiar dumpy brown bottle and supported by its memorable advertising slogan 'Don't be vague, ask for Haig', struggled to maintain its No.1 position and was eventually toppled by the emerging brands of Bell's and Teacher's.

For six years between 1986 and 1994 the UK rights to the brand were transferred to Whyte & Mackay and the brand was re-packaged in a clear bottle. The familiar dumpy brown bottle was consigned to history. Current worldwide sales are above half a million cases but alas in Britain there is very little demand for this once giant brand.

Dimple

Over half a million cases of this de luxe blend are sold each year around the world. George Ogilvy Haig introduced the unique bottle shape in 1893. Part of the attraction of the bottle was its use after the contents had been consumed. Model enthusiasts used them to construct the 'ship-in-the-bottle', the thrifty used them to collect the old silver three-penny pieces and other small coins, and many an empty bottle found its way into living rooms used as the base for a table lamp. In the United States the brand is sold as Pinch and in 1958 it was the first bottle to be patented. The wire

A pleasure that has grown steadily for over three centuries... to receive a bottle of Pinch...so... Don't be vague... Give Haig & Haig

net around the bottle, which was specially made in France, was introduced to prevent the cork stopper from becoming loose whilst being shipped to export markets. The introduction of a new closure in 1973 meant a narrower neck to the bottle and the end of the Dimple piggy bank. The gilded wire-mesh net was abandoned at the same time.

Dimple was one of a number of brands removed by DCL from the British market between 1977 and 1983 to counter difficulties of trading at different prices in the European market. In 1988 the brand experienced a makeover and as well as increasing the age of Dimple from fifteen to eighteen years, the wire net was restored.

1838 GLEN ORD (Highland)

Muir of Ord is fifteen miles north of Inverness in an area with a long history of both illicit and legal distilling. This is Mackenzie country and Thomas Mackenzie, having inherited land in the area in 1820, sought to improve the prosperity of its inhabitants and encouraged the setting up of a number of small distilleries to use all the barley produced locally. Built on the site of an illicit still and sharing land with a mill making oatmeal that had been in existence since 1549, Ord distillery was licensed in 1838 to Donald McLennan and Robert Johnstone. Towards the end of the nineteenth century the whisky blenders James Watson & Sons Ltd of Dundee bought the distillery. When in 1923, as the result of restrictions placed on distilling during the First World War, Watson's business failed, John Dewar & Sons Ltd bought the company and thus when they merged two years later with DCL, Ord's future was assured.

Ord, benefiting from major reconstruction and re-equipping during the period of expansion in the 1960s, is one of the group's larger distilleries with six stills and the capacity to produce around three million litres of pure alcohol in a year. In 1968, DCL built on land adjacent to the distillery a large commercial drum maltings that supplies the malt requirements of nine distilleries in northern Scotland. Heather is added in the malting of the barley destined for the Glen Ord malt whisky and this imparts something of a dry, rooty flavour.

The malt whisky produced by Ord distillery has variously been known as Glenoran, Ord, Muir of Ord and Glenordie. For the last few years the distillery and the malt whisky made in it both enjoy the same name, Glen Ord.

1839 DALMORE (Highland)

The distillery was built in 1839 on land known as Ardross Farm, owned by Alexander Matheson, a partner in the Hong Kong firm of Jardine Matheson. One of the first tenants to operate the distillery was Margaret Sutherland, a 'sometime distiller'. Dalmore is believed to have been the first malt whisky exported to Australia in 1870.

By the time of Barnard's visit in 1887 the distillery had 'been frequently enlarged to meet the growing demand for the Whisky therein manufactured'. The distillery is beautifully situated on the northern shore of the Cromarty Firth, looking south to the rich and fertile Black Isle. Barnard recorded that the distillery 'is favourably situated, having a branch line from the railway running into the premises, and sea communication almost at its doors; added to this, it is placed in the centre of a good barley-growing district, and there is an abundant supply of fine peats in the district.'

The Mackenzie brothers had been tenants since 1878 and the 1886 Crofters Act enabled them to purchase the distillery. The Admiralty took over the distillery during the First World War to make deep-sea mines. It was handed back in 1920 and after a number of buildings damaged by explosions had been repaired, distilling resumed in 1922.

In 1960 the Mackenzies amalgamated their business with their main customer, the Glasgow blending firm Whyte & Mackay. Dalmore is a large distillery and squeezed into two adjoining still houses are eight stills that are the most remarkable in the industry. The wash stills are unusual in having the top of the swan necks sliced off to facilitate their installation. Each of the spirit stills has a copper-clad cooling jacket to encourage the reflux and thus produce a lighter spirit. One of the spirit stills dates back to 1874 and the overall appearance of this fascinating collection of stills has been likened to the trumpets of daffodils or the chimney stacks of old steam locomotives! Much of the spirit is matured in sherry wood and Dalmore 12-year-old is a medium bodied velvety malt, full of flavour with a long lingering aftertaste. Dalmore is one of those very fine malt whiskies that deserve to be discovered by more of the serious drinkers of single malts.

Whyte & Mackay Special Reserve

Charles Mackay and James Whyte went into partnership in 1882 as bonded warehousemen and whisky merchants in Glasgow and they were soon to launch a blended whisky, 'Whyte & Mackay Special'. A strong export business was developed in the English-speaking countries of the world and after the Second World War

THE DISTILLERIES

Far left: *Detail from a wall painting of Dalmore.*

Left: *The stills at Dalmore are the most remarkable in the industry. This spirit still has a copper-clad cooling jacket above the boil pot to encourage refluxing and the making of a lighter spirit.*

Below: *Glen Grant's fine set of stills.*

they made a considerable effort to capture a significant share of the home market. With worldwide sales of a million cases a year, Whyte & Mackay is unusual in being blended in a process known as *double-marrying*. This is where over thirty different malts ranging in age from four to eight years are vatted together and then matured further in casks for a period of eight months. The contents of these are then disgorged and in order to make the final blend, a separate blend is added of up to six grain whiskies, themselves already having been married together for three months. The whole blend is then put back into casks for a further four-month period of marrying prior to being bottled.

1840 GLEN GRANT (Highland-Speyside)

An Elgin lawyer, James Grant, in partnership with his younger brother John, leased Drumbain farm from the Earl of Seafield and in 1839 began building the first distillery in Rothes. They were

attracted to the area by the abundant water supply from the Caperdonich well and the proximity of the Back Burn. Distilling began in 1840 and the distillery was initially known as Drumbain. In 1872 James Grant died and was succeeded by his son, Major James Grant. The distillery was by then one of the largest in Scotland and it was further developed as demand for Glen Grant single malt whisky grew both at home and overseas. The demand was such that Major Grant built a new distillery, Glen Grant No.2, across the road from the original distillery. It was in production for only four years as its opening coincided with the Pattison Crash of 1898 and it was to remain closed for over sixty years before re-opening in 1965 as the **Caperdonich** distillery.

In 1931 Major Grant was succeeded as chairman by his grandson, Major Douglas Mackessack. During his forty-seven years as chairman, Mackessack saw Glen Grant become one of the largest selling single malts in the world with Glen Grant 5-year-old enjoying phenomenal success in Italy. His company merged with two other Speyside distillery companies to become The **Glenlivet**

Distillers Ltd, and he retired in 1978 when the company became part of Seagram Co. Ltd of Canada.

Glen Grant is one of the largest distilleries producing over five million litres of pure alcohol in a year. There are four pairs of stills and the wash stills have an unusual appearance with the base of the neck rising with vertical sides, resembling perhaps the outline of a German military helmet! All stills are fitted with a purifier on the lyne arm and the lighter spirit produced makes Glen Grant single malt one of the lightest in colour and taste of all Highland whiskies. It has a clean and distinctive flavour, slightly dry at first leading to a characteristic fruity finish.

Visitors to Glen Grant distillery have a very special added bonus, the remarkable Glen Grant Garden. First laid out by Major Grant in 1886 in the sheltered glen behind the distillery, this substantial garden extending to twenty-seven acres has recently been carefully restored to its original design and splendour.

1843 GLENMORANGIE (Highland)

Located on the southern shore of Dornoch Firth close to Tain, one of Scotland's oldest Royal Burghs, the distillery began its licensed activity in 1843. It had originally been the Morangie brewery, dating back to 1738, and it was converted for the purposes of distilling by William Matherson and his brother John. The Mathersons lacked capital and the first two stills installed in the distillery were bought second-hand from a gin distillery and were unusually tall.

In 1887 the business that had been dissolved a few years previous was incorporated as the Glenmorangie Distillery Co. Ltd and the distillery was rebuilt. It was the first distillery to use internal steam-heated coils in the new stills and from an early start with the export of Glenmorangie the whisky was widely available overseas by the outbreak of the First World War.

At the end of that war the distillery was sold to its largest customer, Macdonald & Muir, the Leith-based whisky blenders. The distillery was closed for a few years in the 1930s and again for three years during the Second World War. The renewed efforts to export after the war created the situation of demand exceeding supply and there were a few years in the late 1970s when Glenmorangie was rationed to customers in Britain. In 1980 the distillery was extensively redeveloped and two stills were added. Again this was insufficient to keep up with demand and a further four stills were added in 1990. The still house is an impressive sight with the eight stills faithfully replicated from the original design, tall and straight, each with a boil pot just above the shoulder to

Glenmorangie's stills are the tallest in the Scotch Whisky industry.

ensure that only the lightest and finest alcohols are released from the still and collected as spirit.

The process water used in the distillation of Glenmorangie's spirit comes from the nearby Tarlogie springs and it has been calculated that it takes one hundred years for the rainwater, from the moment it hits earth, to find its way through a long and tortuous underground journey to the springs. During this long period of time the water picks up many flavoursome ingredients and is both rich in minerals leached from the local red sandstone and, unusually, very hard, seeping as it does through an underground bed of limestone.

It is not only the water that has a history of one hundred years. Glenmorangie has long prided itself in its 'wood management policy' to ensure that the casks used to mature Glenmorangie's spirit are made of the best American white oak. Centurion oak trees on the cool north-facing slopes of the Ozark Mountains in Missouri are felled, the wood is cut into staves and air dried for eighteen months and then made into casks and leased to Heaven Hill Bourbon of Kentucky for their fill of Bourbon. When emptied, these casks are shipped to Scotland, filled with Glenmorangie spirit and allowed to rest and mature in one of the distillery's traditional earth floored *dunnage* warehouses for at least ten years.

Glenmorangie's policy is to use only American oak in the making of their main style of single malt. In recent years they have introduced a 'Wood Finish' range where the generic 10-year-old is racked into casks which have previously contained port, sherry or madeira, for a further and final period of maturation when extra dimensions are added of colour, nose, taste and finish.

Glenmorangie is a big brand on the international scene. It is the fourth largest worldwide and has held the No.1 position in Scotland for many years. To preserve its exclusive position in the industry, Glenmorangie is never sold as such to blenders. If blenders require Glenmorangie single malt they can only buy it with a small addition of **Glen Moray** single malt and it is then known as Westport, a *vatted* rather than a single malt.

A final point on pronunciation. The preferred way is Glenmorangie, to be said as in orange!

1845 ROYAL LOCHNAGAR (Highland)

A former illicit distiller, James Robertson of Crathie, built the first licensed Lochnagar distillery in 1826 on the north side of the River Dee. In 1841 rival unlicensed distillers burned it down and a new distillery was built four years later by John Begg on a site on the south bank of the Dee near Balmoral Castle. Begg called his distillery New Lochnagar. In 1848, shortly after Queen Victoria had taken up residence at Balmoral, she paid a visit to the distillery accompanied by her consort, Prince Albert. The visit was a success and a few days later John Begg was delighted to have been awarded the grant of a Royal Warrant of Appointment as a supplier to the Queen and the distillery was immediately renamed Royal Lochnagar. By the time of Begg's death in 1880 he had developed a large trade in blended whisky at home and abroad. The distillery remained in the ownership of the Begg family until 1916 when DCL, seeking to enlarge its export trade in blended whisky, acquired all the shares owned by the Begg family.

The distillery is built in attractive red granite and it was re-equipped in 1963, retaining to this day the feel and atmosphere of a Victorian distillery. It possesses one of few remaining examples of open mash tuns in the industry, complete with the traditional rakes, and uses four rather than the usual three waters in the mashing cycle. The stills are small and each has its own cast-iron worm tub.

The distillery's proximity to the Royal residence guarantees a regular flow of visitors through the distillery. The shop at Royal Lochnagar has a large range of rare and special malts of the recently enlarged Diageo group, many of which are at cask strength and a number are from distilleries closed by the old Distillers Company in the 1980s.

With its two small stills Royal Lochnagar's still house is compact and of smart appearance.

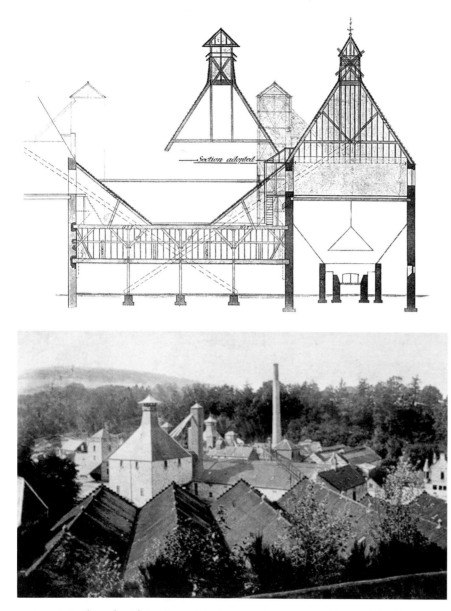

Top: *Doig's plans for alterations at Dailuaine incorporate his new idea for a pagoda style of ventilator above the kiln. It was successful and became the standard design for all future kiln roofs.*

Above: *Dailuaine as it appeared on an old postcard of 1905.*

Opposite: *A delivery of empty casks by sea in exchange for a consignment of Caol Ila's whisky to the blenders on mainland Scotland. This was a typical scene in the 1960s.*

1846 CAOL ILA (Islay)

Attracted by the excellent supply of water from the Loch nam Ban (the lady's loch), Caol Ila was built by Hector Henderson in 1846. As with all other distilleries on Islay, Caol Ila is located right on the edge of the sea and, with difficult access, a steep and winding road was built down to the site of the new distillery from the track leading to Port Askaig. The business failed in 1854 and for a brief period the owner of the Isle of Jura distillery ran Caol Ila. In 1863, Bulloch Lade, a successful Glasgow firm of whisky traders, acquired and expanded the distillery and built a new pier to allow ships to bring in empty casks, barley and coal and to take away casks of whisky.

Barnard wondered at the magnificent siting of the distillery, 'it stands in the wildest and most picturesque locality we have seen. It is situated on the Sound of Islay on the very verge of the sea, in a deep recess in the mountain, mostly cut out of the solid rock'.

Caol Ila was absorbed into DCL in 1930 and the distillery was closed for most of the 1930s and again during the war. Caol Ila was completely rebuilt between 1972 and 1974 and the design and materials of the finished building have been much criticised as being totally unsympathetic and in sharp contrast with the remarkable beauty of the area surrounding it. However, the distillery does have one redeeming feature. The views from the windows of the concrete and glass still house, with its six large handsome stills, across the Sound of Islay to the Paps of Jura, are undoubtedly the best of any distillery in Scotland.

An interesting development took place at Caol Ila in the mid-1990s. The new spirit is no longer matured in the warehouses but is sent in bulk by road tanker to Central Scotland where it is filled into casks and matured there. Although little of Caol Ila is available as a single malt, it will be interesting to see what, if any, effect maturation on the mainland will have on a whisky that has traditionally been matured in warehouses built on the edge of the sea.

1851 DAILUAINE (Highland-Speyside)

In 1851 William Mackenzie, a local farmer, established a small distillery in a hollow by the Carron Burn and named it Dailuaine, which in Gaelic means the 'green vale'. The distillery was to remain in the control of the Mackenzie family until the death of the founder's son, Thomas, in 1915. In the mid-1880s, after the distillery had been substantially rebuilt and enlarged, Dailuaine had become one of the largest in the Highlands. Mackenzie & Co.

became a limited company in 1891 and in 1898 amalgamated with **Talisker** and the neighbouring Imperial distillery that had been built by Thomas Mackenzie in 1897. The new company, Dailuaine-Talisker Distilleries Ltd, of which Mackenzie was chairman, had been formed at the peak of prosperity in the whisky industry. The company like so many others was to suffer badly as a result of the collapse of Pattison's and it struggled to survive during the years leading up to the outbreak of the First World War.

When Mackenzie died in 1915, and with no family to succeed him, a group of major customers tried to guide the company out of difficulty. In 1925 this consortium of John Dewar, James Buchanan, the Distillers Company and John Walker amalgamated to form an enlarged Distillers Company with Dailuaine-Talisker retained as a subsidiary company.

The distillery was to benefit from its closeness to the Strathspey Railway that had by 1863 reached Carron, less than a mile from the distillery. It did however take a further forty-two years before a short length of branch line was built into the distillery.

Dailuaine suffered a major fire in 1917 and it was to take three years before the distillery could be re-opened. One loss in that fire was the pagoda roof. This loss was significant because it was the first such example of this style of roof designed by the architect and distillery engineer, Charles Chree Doig. Born in 1855 and working from his office in Elgin, Doig was responsible for the design of many of the new distilleries on Speyside during the boom years at the end of the nineteenth century. It was at a site meeting in May 1889 at Dailuaine, to discuss plans for alterations to the maltings and kiln, that Doig scrapped his original design of the kiln's ventilator and he incorporated the design of the roof of the Chinese pagoda. This strikingly attractive design, which he called the 'Doig Ventilator', was based on the architectural detail of the golden pagoda and had the practical effect of producing a stronger draw for the peat fire.

The distillery was expanded in 1960 to have six stills. Little of its production is bottled as a single malt, the bulk of Dailuaine's make is used in Diageo's range of blended whiskies.

Imperial

Designed by Charles Doig, Imperial was unusual in being built of red Aberdeen brick. To commemorate the fact that the distillery was completed in 1897, the year of Queen Victoria's Diamond Jubilee, one of the malting kilns was capped with a massive imperial crown that survived until the distillery was rebuilt in 1955.

Only two years after Imperial was completed it fell silent for twenty years. When DCL became its owners in 1925, the distillery,

which had been re-opened in 1919, was promptly closed and remained silent for a further thirty years. Imperial was rebuilt and re-opened in 1955 and enlarged in 1965 with the addition of a second pair of stills. DCL closed the distillery in 1985 and four years later sold it to Allied Distillers Ltd who re-opened it, only to close it again in 1998. Closed for a longer period than when it was actually in production, Imperial distillery is unlikely to re-open.

1869 CRAGGANMORE
(Highland-Speyside)

In 1869, John Smith having already managed **Macallan**, **Glenfarclas** and **Glenlivet** distilleries, obtained a lease from Sir George Macpherson Grant of Ballindalloch Castle to set up his own distilling operation on Ayeon Farm on the Ballindalloch estate. Situated close to the River Spey, Cragganmore was the first Speyside distillery to be built adjacent to the new railway line and therefore to take advantage of this new system of transport. In 1887, a 'whisky special' departed from Ballindalloch station with twenty-five wagons fully loaded with casks containing 16,000 gallons of whisky bound for Aberdeen and then on to James Watson, whisky merchants and blenders in Dundee.

John Smith died in 1886 and his brother George took control of the distillery until 1893 when John's son, Gordon was old enough to take over the business. The distillery was unaffected by the

Far left: *A 1903 postcard shows Imperial's splendid crown that was to witness the distillery's closure for all but seven of its first fifty-seven years of life.*

Left: Entrance to *Cragganmore.*

Below: *Note the unusual design of the top of Cragganmore's spirit still. Variations on this unusual design are also found at Pulteney and Dalmore.*

Pattison's crash in 1898 because all of Cragganmore's output was required for blending by James Watson. Proof of the distillery's success at a time when much of the industry was floundering was a complete reconstruction in 1902 with Charles Doig as architect.

When the lease expired in 1923, the distillery was sold to the Cragganmore-Glenlivet Distillery Co. Ltd, a company equally owned by the Ballindalloch Estate and White Horse Distillers. DCL took over White Horse's 50% share of the business in 1925 and it was to take a further forty years before DCL acquired the balance of the shares to take full control of Cragganmore. In 1964 the distillery was doubled in size with the addition of a second pair of stills. The spirit stills retain the unusual feature from the original design by John Smith in having flat tops to the necks and this is another distillery to use worms rather than condensers.

Cragganmore 12-year-old, with its complex nose, firm body and malty smoky finish, was selected as the representative of Speyside in Diageo's range of Classic Malts.

1871 INCHGOWER (Highland-Speyside)

Inchgower is a short distance from the sea on the outskirts of the small fishing town of Buckie and is one of three distilleries to be classified as Speyside *and* coastal. The other two are **Macduff**, near Banff, and Glenglassaugh, near Portsoy, owned by Highland Distillers and mothballed since 1986.

The copy line 'Afore ye go', appearing in this 1937 advertisement, was to stand the test of time and to be an integral part of the successful development of Bell's whisky over the next fifty years.

Alexander Wilson built the distillery in 1871 to replace his original very small distillery, Tochineal, some ten miles west near Cullen. Inchgower was built on a grand scale with the distillery, carpenter's shop, cooperage, smiddy and warehouses grouped around a quadrangle and a row of distillery workers' houses leading out to the main road. The distillery remained in the

hands of the Wilson family until the business went bankrupt in 1929. In 1933 the local Buckie council bought the distillery and the Wilson family home, Arradoul House, for £1,000 and three years later sold it to Arthur Bell & Sons for £3,000. Two additional stills were added in 1966, doubling the output of the distillery. After being taken over by Guinness in 1985 and merging with Grand Metropolitan in 1997, Inchgower is one of Diageo's twenty-seven malt whisky distilleries in Scotland.

1876 GLENLOSSIE (Highland-Speyside)

In 1876, the year that Graham Alexander Bell invented the telephone, John Duff, who had for a number of years been manager of **Glendronach** distillery, built Glenlossie distillery three miles south of Elgin. His company was liquidated in 1896 and it was reformed as Glenlossie-Glenlivet Distillery Co. Ltd. In the same year a private siding was completed to link the distillery with the main Elgin to Perth railway line at Longmorn, two miles away. When Glenlossie reopened in 1919 after two years closure during the Great War, Scottish Malt Distillers bought a controlling interest in the distillery, its first such purchase of a Highland malt whisky distillery. Apart from a serious fire in 1929, when a horse-drawn fire engine of 1869 vintage was used to fight the fire, the distillery has had an uneventful and steady history. It was developed and expanded in the 1950s and again in 1962 when a third pair of stills was added. The three spirit stills are fitted with purifiers to produce a lighter spirit and the malt whisky from Glenlossie is a key element in a number of Diageo's blends.

In 1971 Glenlossie's owners, Scottish Malt Distillers, built a new distillery, **Mannochmore**, on an adjacent site.

1878 GLENBURGIE (Highland-Speyside)

In 1810, on a site near Alves, six miles west of Elgin, William Paul established a small distillery that he called Kilnflat. The distillery fell into disuse around 1870 and one small building that was probably the still house has survived to the present day.

The distillery was revived in 1878 by Charles Kay and given the name of Glenburgie. After two changes of ownership, the company was liquidated in 1925 and fell silent until 1936 when Hiram Walker-Gooderham Worts of Ontario bought it along with **Miltonduff** distillery, located a few miles to the east near Elgin. Following the merger in 1987 of Hiram Walker into Allied Lyons plc (now Allied Distillers) the malt whisky produced at Glenburgie continues to be a fingerprint malt in the Ballantine's blend.

Between 1958 and 1981 Glenburgie was home to two Lomond stills and the single malt whisky produced from them was known as Glencraig.

1878 GLENROTHES (Highland-Speyside)

Established in 1878 on the site of a sawmill on the banks of the Burn of Rothes, the distillery was completed in May of the following year. James Stuart & Co., leaseholders of **Macallan** distillery, had carried out the first phase of the construction of Glenrothes. Following the departure of James Stuart, a consortium of three local businessmen took over the construction and facing financial difficulties the distillery was built to a much smaller design than had originally been planned. There was also considerable wrangling over the rights to the distillery's water supply with the neighbouring distillery, **Glen Spey**, being built at the same time by none less than the same James Stuart!

Highland Distilleries was established in 1887 out of the amalgamation of Glenrothes and **Bunnahabhain** distillery on Islay and the future of Glenrothes distillery was assured. The distillery was doubled in size in 1898 and has had an uneventful career apart from a fire in May 1922 when two and a half thousand casks of whisky were destroyed in one of the distillery's warehouses. Few changes were made to the distillery until 1963 when the distillery was overhauled and two stills were added, making six in total. A new still house, clad in attractive smooth red granite, was completed in 1980 and eight stills were installed with a further two stills fitted in 1989. This is one of the industry's largest distilleries with an ability to produce between five and six million litres of pure alcohol in a year. Much of what is produced finds its way into Cutty Sark and The Famous Grouse.

Cutty Sark Blended Scots Whisky

Berry Bros & Rudd Ltd is a wine and spirit merchant of great age and reputation. It remains a family firm with its roots going back to 1698 since when it has occupied the same premises in London's St James's Street. In 1923, the firm's partners set about to produce a new blend of whisky made from only the highest quality malt and grain whiskies and of a natural light colour. They sought the advice and assistance of the Scottish artist James McBey and it was he who designed the label depicting the *Cutty Sark*, the fastest clipper ship ever built. The light colour and mellow character of the blend

Glenrothes distillery in the late 1890s with the still house and worm tubs behind the chimney and the kiln behind the three malt barns.

The view from the still house at Glenrothes distillery is somewhat different from that enjoyed at Jura!

Left: *James McBey's intention was to have on the label the* Cutty Sark *clipper in full sail set against a background 'yellowed with age'. A printer's error produced a bright canary yellow background that delighted the Berry partners and was accepted.*

helped establish the popularity of the brand in the American market during the period of Prohibition. In 1961 Cutty Sark became the first brand to sell more than one million cases in the USA. It continues to be a popular brand in the States and sells well in Europe and Japan with total annual export sales of two million cases.

1878 GLEN SPEY (Highland-Speyside)

James Stuart was a corn merchant and, in addition to his interests in **Macallan** and **Glenrothes** distilleries, he added in 1878 a distilling operation to his oatmeal mill, the Mills of Rothes and this was to be known as Glen Spey distillery.

In 1887, the year of the Golden Jubilee, Stuart sold the distillery to W. & A. Gilbey of London for £11,000. Gilbey's had been in business for thirty years and had developed a thriving business selling wines, cognac, other spirits and liqueurs. Familiar with the excellence and remarkable growth in the sales of whisky and pursuing a policy of cutting out the middleman, they took the decision to become the first English company to buy a malt whisky distillery. Eight years later they bought **Strathmill** and in 1903 they added **Knockando** to their Speyside collection of distilleries.

Apart from a warehouse roof collapsing in 1892 as a result of a very heavy fall of snow and a fire in 1920 which was kept clear of

Above: *Glen Spey Six Years Old Pure Malt Whisky was being sold at 3s 6d per bottle (17½p) in 1903.*

Right: *An advertisement for Gilbey's Spey Royal in the* New Yorker *in June 1950 at the time when W. & A. Gilbey was an independent company.*

the still house and warehouses, Glen Spey has had a steady untroubled career. The distillery underwent a major rebuild in 1970; two stills were added to double the capacity and a semi-Lauter mash tun was installed. This mash tun had been developed by New Mill Engineering of Elgin and was the first of its type in the industry and mash tuns of a similar construction are referred to as the 'Glen Spey'. The spirit stills are fitted with purifiers and are somewhat unusually installed outside the still house.

Glen Spey is rarely seen as a single malt. It has long been associated with the blends of Spey Royal and J&B Rare.

1879 ABERLOUR (Highland-Speyside)

The village of Aberlour on the south side of the River Spey is a perfect example of the traditional Scottish Highland village. The local Laird, Charles Grant, started to build the new village of Charlestown of Aberlour in 1812 and it has developed to be the home of the family-owned firm making the world famous Walker's shortbread. It is also the home of a distillery built in 1879 by James Fleming, a local banker and grain merchant, who had for a few years leased **Dailuaine** distillery. Fleming's distillery replaced a small one built in 1826 a mile or so upstream from the present location.

Barnard thought Aberlour to be 'a charming village' and the distillery, 'built on the banks of the Lour, about 300 yards from the noble river Spey' to be 'a perfect model distillery . . . with no steam power . . . the continuous flow of water being sufficient to drive all the machinery'.

In 1892 Fleming sold the distillery to Robert Thorne & Sons of Greenock, a successful firm of whisky blenders who immediately set about to improve the distillery's equipment and build more warehouses. In January 1898, there was a major fire and the architect Doig was commissioned to rebuild and extend the distillery. Production resumed in late summer only months before the Pattison's crash. After the First World War, Thorne's sold Aberlour to a brewing company, W.H. Holt from Chorlton-cum-Hardy near Manchester, who kept the distillery in production until the Second World War.

At the end of the war, S. Campbell & Sons Ltd became the distillery's new owners and steadily updated the equipment and the distillery's output. In 1974, a year after a major rebuilding of the distillery, Pernod Ricard became the first French drinks company to make a direct investment in the distilling of Scotch whisky by buying the House of Campbell and thus gave the distillery a very confident platform for its future.

Aberlour has survived but R. Thorne's Greenock distillery portrayed on this postcard from 1912 closed permanently in 1915.

1881 BUNNAHABHAIN (Islay)

In 1881, on a very remote stretch of the east coast of Islay where the river Margadale flows into the Sound of Islay, two local farmers, the Greenlees brothers, built Bunnahabhain distillery. Built from locally quarried stone, the distillery was built to produce a high volume of malt whisky suitable for the blending market in Glasgow. In 1887 they amalgamated their company, the Islay Distillery Co.

Ltd with William Grant & Co., owners of **Glenrothes**-Glenlivet to form the Highland Distilleries Co. Ltd.

At about the same time Barnard visited the distillery and commented that the last mile of road to the distillery

leads in serpentine curves downwards to the bay. This road was entirely constructed by the company, and is as good as it was costly; but, although indispensable, the greater proportion of it is not much

Top: *Bunnahabhain in the 1950s.*

Above: *Bunnahabhain warehouses on the water's edge.*

Right: *Bunnahabhain's stills are very large and the spirit still in the foreground is of an unusual bulbous shape with its great onion base leading up into a broad swan neck.*

used for heavy traffic, the extensive import and export being entirely by sea. The Company have several steamers constantly chartered for the purpose of carrying barley and coals, while Mr MacBrayne's steamer 'Islay' calls weekly with general stores, and loads whisky for the return voyage. To enable the work of loading and discharging to be expeditiously performed, the company have erected a commodious and handsome pier at a cost of about £3,500 . . . The distillery proper is a fine pile of buildings in the form of a square and quite enclosed. Entering by a noble gateway one forms an immediate sense of compactness and symmetrical construction of the work.

Barnard noted that 'Neat villas have been erected … for the Excise Officers and two large ranges of houses provide ample accommodation for the workmen. A Reading Room and School Room have likewise, with praiseworthy liberality, been provided by the Company.…There are fifty to seventy hands employed throughout the season.'

In the first full season of distilling (1882-1883), there was a shortage of suitable Scottish malting barley and supplies were brought in from Denmark, Poland and Russia.

A hundred years later, the distillery was closed for a two-year period as a result of overproduction in the industry.

Bunnahabhain can produce two-and-a-half million litres of pure alcohol and does so by the use of some impressive equipment. The mash tun is very big, taking 13.5 tonnes of barley in each mash. The six Oregon pine wash backs are also large each with a capacity of 66,500 litres. The unusual onion-shaped stills look and are enormous. The wash stills each have a capacity of 35,300 litres and are believed to be the largest in Scotland.

Bunnahabhain, which is Gaelic for 'mouth of the river', was first bottled by its owners in 1960. The process water is very light in peat flavour and the result is a full bodied whisky with a light Islay medicinal flavour and a good fruity background. Bunnahabhain is probably the malt that is the least typical of the malt whisky drinker's perception of what to expect of Islay's malts. That is not a problem, Bunnahabhain 12-year-old is a very approachable single malt. The distillery was sold in 2003 to Burn Stewart Distillers.

1881 BRUICHLADDICH (Islay)

William, John and Robert Harvey built Bruichladdich, Scotland's most westerly distillery, in 1881 and, like all other distilleries on Islay, it was situated next to the sea with fine views south over Loch Indaal to Bowmore. During the depression years of 1929 to 1937

the distillery fell silent and remained in the hands of the Harvey family until 1938 when they sold it to Joseph Hobbs who added the distillery to the collection owned by The National Distillers of America. Bruichladdich had new owners in 1952, 1960 and again in 1968 when the distillery became part of the Invergordon Distillers group which had been established in 1960 as part of the Hawker Siddeley Group. Whilst under American ownership Whyte & Mackay bought Invergordon in 1993 and closed Bruichladdich two years later because of over-capacity in the enlarged group. During its six years of closure the distillery was re-opened on two occasions to distill a small quantity of spirit and thus maintain continuity of supply in the years to come.

The future of this delightful distillery looked increasingly dismal until, at the end of 2000, it was announced that Murray, McDavid Ltd, an independent whisky company leading a consortium of business interests including a number based on Islay had bought the distillery. After considerable and totally sympathetic restoration of the distillery and its equipment, Bruichladdich, to a fanfare of appreciation, was brought back to life in May 2001.

The distillery oozes character with its open-topped mash tun complete with the traditional raking system, its cast-iron brewing tanks dating back to the year of the distillery's construction, its four tall and slender stills and its warehouses with their traditional earth floors.

Many words have been used to describe the delightful taste and character of Bruichladdich. Using virtually unpeated water from the hills behind the distillery, Bruichladdich is a smooth and delicate whisky with some spiciness and a sweet nutty character.

Above: *Many items of distillery equipment at Bruichladdich date back to 1881. This brewing tank containing the hot water for mashing is one such example.*

Above: *This old warehouse, now housing Bruichladdich's bottling plant, opened in May 2003. There are only two other distilleries that bottle their own malt whiskies: Glenfiddich and Springbank.*

Right: *The warm sweet smell from Bruichladdich's open mash tun is one of the welcome signs that the distillery has been brought back to life!*

There are many plans to develop further the potential of this gem of distilleries. There will be a new heavily peated style, to be known as Port Charlotte. The first spirit is already being matured in the old warehouses of the eponymous distillery closed in 1929, to be found two miles along the road to the west of Bruichladdich.

There is every sign that the enthusiasm and optimism of Bruichladdich's new owners will bring the distillery the solid and successful future that it deserves.

1887 GLENFIDDICH (Highland-Speyside)

During the twenty years that William Grant worked at the **Mortlach** distillery he developed a strong personal interest in building one of his own. In 1886, at the age of forty-seven, with his nine children and one stonemason, he set about fulfilling his ambition. He paid £119 19s 10d (£119.99) for some old distilling equipment and second-hand stills that were being replaced by Mrs Cumming at Cardow (**Cardhu**) distillery. Taking about a year to complete the building of Glenfiddich distillery and at a total cost of about £800, the first malting commenced on 15 November 1887 and the first spirit ran from the stills on Christmas Day in that special year, the Golden Jubilee of Queen Victoria.

The rapid growth of blended whiskies and the building of distilleries on Speyside encouraged a speculator to attempt to buy the land adjacent to Glenfiddich on which to build a distillery. Concerned that this would have meant sharing the water rights with the new distillery, Grant responded by putting in an offer for the land and its water rights. The offer was successful and he immediately set about building a second distillery and by the end of 1898 his new **Balvenie** distillery was in production.

When Pattison's of Leith, Glenfiddich's largest customer, collapsed in 1898, William Grant reacted to the enormity of the problem by deciding firstly to produce his own blended whisky, 'Standfast', secondly to act as wholesalers selling direct to the retailers and thirdly to explore the possibilities of exporting overseas. The company survived the aftermath of Pattison's and

Right: *An early twentieth-century advertisement for Grant's Stand Fast Scotch Whisky.*

Far right: *Glenfiddich – The world's largest selling brand of single malt Scotch whisky.*

TIME AND CRAFTSMANSHIP

developed a strong trade for their products in Scotland and England and steadily established a solid network of overseas agents and distributors.

In line with all other distilleries Grants did not distill in the two years 1917 to 1919 but shortly after the end of the war production was back to normal. With renewed optimism about the future, Charles Grant, now in charge of the company and needing extra production capacity to satisfy the needs of his customers, bought **Glendronach** distillery, near Huntly. The company ran the distillery for forty years until selling it to William Teacher & Sons in 1960.

Grant's Standfast has in recent years been renamed William Grant's Family Reserve and still commands very strong worldwide sales in excess of four million cases.

During the 1960s the Grant's had the foresight and determination to market and support the sales on a worldwide basis of Glenfiddich single malt whisky in its unique and now very familiar green triangular bottle, first introduced in 1957. Over one in five of all bottles of single malt whisky sold throughout the world is Glenfiddich. For many years it has been the largest selling brand and in recent years annual sales have exceeded 800,000 cases. In 1974, William Grant's was the first company in the UK to be awarded with the Queen's Award to Industry for outstanding Export Achievement.

Glenfiddich is the largest single malt whisky distillery in Scotland with a capacity to produce ten million litres of alcohol in a year. It has two large mash tuns, twenty-four Douglas fir wash backs and two still houses equipped with ten wash and eighteen spirit stills. All the stills are small, heated by coal-fired direct flame, and the wash stills are fitted with rummagers. This is the only distillery in the Highlands to bottle its own whisky, a special feature shared at present only with Springbank distillery in Campbeltown.

The company owns 1,200 acres of farmland over the water source, the Robbie Dubh well, and by controlling the agricultural methods used, the quality and purity of the water supply is guaranteed.

The distillery was the first to be seriously interested in welcoming visitors to see how malt whisky is made. The visitor centre was opened in 1969 and currently attracts around 100,000 people each year.

The standard Glenfiddich is an uncomplicated malt with a light and delicate character which often appeals to those seeking an introduction to single malt whisky. In recent years the company has developed a number of very attractive mature expressions of Glenfiddich, which have attracted the interest of experienced aficionados of the malt whiskies from Speyside's Golden Triangle.

The rebuilding programme of the 1960s brought Craigellachie's distilling equipment up to date at the expense of the distillery's good Victorian looks.

1891 CRAIGELLACHIE
(Highland-Speyside)

The Craigellachie Distillery Co. was established in 1888 by a partnership of whisky blenders and merchants led by Alexander Edward, owner of **Benrinnes** distillery, and Peter Mackie of Mackie and Co., owners of **Lagavulin**. The distillery, designed by Charles Doig, was completed in 1891 and under the sole proprietorship of Mackie's. It was well located near to the railway station at Craigellachie Junction with connections to Elgin, Aberdeen and the south. Rail transport ceased to be used by the distillery in 1967 and the line closed the following year.

When Peter Mackie died in 1924 his company was re-named White Horse Distillers and was amalgamated into DCL in 1927. Craigellachie remained in that group until 1998 when, following the merger of DCL's owners Guinness with Grand Metropolitan to create the giant drinks company Diageo, Craigellachie along with **Aberfeldy**, **Brackla** and **Aultmore** and the company of John Dewar & Sons Ltd were all sold to Bacardi.

In 1964-1965 a large part of the distillery was rebuilt. A second pair of stills was added and the worm tub system of condensing the spirit was retained. The distillery is built on a spectacular site on a spur of a hill overlooking the small village of Craigellachie and the confluence of the Rivers Spey and Fiddich. It is however a surprise to the regular travellers on the Rothes to Dufftown road to see after many years the bold lettering on the wall of the still house now no longer reads **WHITE HORSE DISTILLERS LIMITED**, but rather **John Dewar & Sons Ltd**! Ah, *plus ça change*!

1891 STRATHMILL
(Highland-Speyside)

Situated on the banks of the river Isla on the outskirts of Keith, a group of buildings previously used as corn and flourmills was converted to form a distillery that was originally known as Glenisla-Glenlivet. In 1895, W. & A. Gilbey of London acquired this, their second distillery, on Speyside and renamed it Strathmill. During its steady history the distillery has been an important constituent malt in Gilbey's range of blended whiskies and during the last thirty years within J&B Rare. Expanded in 1968 with the addition of a second pair of stills, the distillery produces a spirit that is light and therefore most appropriate to the style of the J&B Rare blend. This is achieved in stills with boil pots at the base of the neck and with purifiers attached to the lyne arms of both spirit stills.

1893 BALVENIE
(Highland-Speyside)

To protect the water rights of his **Glenfiddich** distillery, William Grant bought the adjacent twelve-acre site. On the land was a derelict eighteenth-century mansion, the New Castle of Balvenie. He decided to build his second distillery and to incorporate the old house into the plans. Balvenie distillery, which was originally to have been called Glen Gordon, took fifteen months to complete under the close supervision of William and his son, John, at a total cost of £2,000. There was a good deal of second-hand equipment in the distillery, including a still that he bought from **Lagavulin** for £47. The first distillation was completed on the first day in May 1893.

The old mansion, which had been converted to house grain storage, maltings and a bonded store for maturing whisky, was demolished in the 1920s and replaced with a new malt barn and kiln. The distillery was expanded in the 1950s and again in the 1960s and now has eight stills. Balvenie is one of the few

Christmas 1971 advertising in the United States at the time when J&B Rare was aiming to become the country's largest selling blended Scotch whisky.

remaining distilleries with its own floor maltings providing about ten per cent of the distillery's needs. Some of the barley is from a very local source, the neighbouring Grant family's farm.

The water source of Balvenie is the same as Glenfiddich, but the malt whisky is quite different.

Balvenie distillery is unique in carrying out the mashing and fermentation on behalf of another distillery owned by Grant's – **Kininvie**!

1894 KNOCKDHU
(Highland-Speyside)

John Morrison bought the Knock estate from the Earl of Fife in 1892 and, discovering a fine supply of spring water on Knock Hill, he sent a sample to analysts in Edinburgh. By coincidence these were the same analysts used by DCL. Not owning a Highland malt whisky distillery at that time, DCL was seeking to satisfy the demand for Highland malt from John Haig & Co., whisky dealers, which had contracted to buy all its supplies of whisky from DCL. Morrison sold the company a site next to the Banff branch of the Great North of Scotland railway line between Aberdeen and Elgin and work on building the distillery began in May 1893. Ideally situated close to the Laich o'Moray, a major area of barley growing, and on the edge of inexhaustible supplies of peat and spring water, the distillery, built in fine grey granite, began production in October 1894.

As a result of the economic depression, the distillery was silent between 1931 and 1933 and again for the war years of 1940 to 1945, when a unit of the Indian Army occupied it. Knockdhu was a casualty of the cutbacks in production by DCL in the early 1980s and was closed in 1983. It was sold to Inver House Distillers in 1988 and reopened the following year. Knockdhu is a distillery of some charm with original Victorian buildings and traditional distilling equipment, such as the copper-domed cast-iron mash tun, wooden wash backs and two fine stills with traditional worm tubs.

Above: *With only two stills Knockdhu's spirit safe is a simple affair.*

Left: *Knockdhu distillery.*

To distinguish the single malt whisky of Knockdhu from that of **Knockando**, it is sold as An Cnoc, the Gaelic for The Knock, the black hill.

1894 LONGMORN (Highland-Speyside)

There had been a grain mill on the site of the distillery since the seventeenth century and there is a belief that the site had also been home to an ancient chapel. Longmorn is the Gaelic for 'the place of the holy man'. John Duff and two partners built the distillery in 1894 and in 1898, when **Benriach** distillery was built on a neighbouring site, the partners bought it and renamed the company Longmorn-Glenlivet Distilleries Co. Ltd. The company through various acquisitions and takeovers became part of Seagram of Canada in 1978.

Longmorn is a large distillery with eight stills and in common with the other distilleries operated by Chivas Brothers sends all its new spirit by tanker to the company's vast filling and warehousing complex in Keith.

1896 TAMDHU (Highland-Speyside)

Charles Doig designed Tamdhu distillery and the building was financed by a group of local businessmen. The distillery was one of three distilleries being built in the same parish at the same time. The others were **Knockando** and the now mothballed Imperial. The first casks were filled on 21 July 1897 and shortly after its first distilling season Tamdhu was bought by Highland Distilleries in whose hands it remains to the present day. In 1927 a combination of poor trading conditions resulting from the world economic recession, and difficulties in disposing of the distillery's effluent, prompted the closure of the distillery and Tamdhu remained closed for over twenty years. A new effluent treatment plant was built in 1947 and the distillery reopened in July of the following year.

The floor maltings were replaced in 1950 with a system that is still in place today. Ten Saladin boxes were built and each can take 22 tonnes of barley. Each of these long concrete boxes is fitted with a mechanical turner that crawls along the length of the box at specified intervals to prevent matting of the sprouting barley rootlets. The floor of each box is perforated and air circulates through the sprouting barley keeping the temperature under control. After five days in these germination units the green malt is transferred to a modern form of kiln. The 'Seager' is a pressure kiln, designed as a large box with air blowing through the malt drying bed. It is able to take 40 tonnes of grain and is self-filling, self-emptying and takes only half the time to dry the grain when compared with the traditional kiln. The distillery produces all of its own requirements of malted barley and any excess is sent to Highland's **Glenrothes** distillery in Rothes. Every effort is made throughout the industry to recycle and reuse any waste heat, but in the 1970s some bizarre experiments were carried out by a number of distilleries to produce a profitable by-product using some of the excess hot air and water. Tamdhu's contribution was the rearing of young trout and salmon. We have already seen **Glen Garioch's** tomatoes and another distillery tried growing orchids!

There were few references to the contribution made to the companies' profits from these ventures! There was even one company that went into a serious attempt at growing mushrooms in one of its warehouses. They learned a sharp lesson that they should not have diversified into farming and stayed with what they knew best – distilling!

Tamdhu was considerably expanded in the early 1970s to accommodate three pairs of stills and now has the capacity to produce over five million litres of alcohol in a year.

Built adjacent to the Strathspey railway line, Tamdhu distillery had its own station originally called Dalbeallie but later renamed Knockando. After the closure of the line in the 1960s, the old railway station was used for a number of years as a visitor centre. The distillery, which was for some time one of the original distilleries on the Spey Whisky Trail, is no longer open to visitors.

In 1976 Tamdhu was made available as an 8-year-old single malt and a few years later this was replaced with a 10-year-old version. The current version has no age statement. The malt produced at Tamdhu has long been associated with the popular blended whisky, The Famous Grouse.

1896 DUFFTOWN (Highland-Speyside)

Peter Mackenzie was already the owner of **Blair Athol** distillery when in 1895, along with several business partners, he converted a sawmill and a meal mill into a distillery and the first spirit flowed from the stills in November 1896. Initially there were a number of disputes with the Cowie family, owners of the neighbouring

Opened as Tamdhu siding in 1896, it was renamed Dalbeallie in 1899 and again re-named Knockando in 1905.

The Scottish background of Bell's Old Scotch Whisky is emphasised in this advertisement from 1990.

Mortlach distillery, over the rights to the water supply. When these matters were resolved, Dufftown distillery steadily produced fine malt whisky used by Mackenzie in his blended whiskies that found a ready market in the United States. However, his business was badly affected by Prohibition and in 1933 he sold both distilleries to Arthur Bell & Sons Ltd of Perth.

The distillery was considerably expanded in the 1960s and 1970s at the time when the Bell's blend was experiencing rapid growth. The distillery is currently undergoing further redevelopment and in the first stage the old maltings were converted into a tun room with the installation of twelve fully-automated stainless-steel wash backs. Dufftown is Diageo's largest distillery capable of producing nearly four million litres of pure alcohol.

1896 ABERFELDY (Highland)

Between 1825 and 1867 there had been a small distillery on the banks of the Pitilie burn which flows into the river Tay, a mile east of the delightful small Highland Perthshire town of Aberfeldy. In 1896, the Dewar's family decided that they needed to build their own distillery to guarantee the supply of a good blending malt whisky, not too assertively peaty nor too light in character, to be used in their White Label blended whisky. The water in the burn was already known to be ideal for distillation so building of John Dewar's distillery adjacent to the Perth to Aberfeldy railway line began in the same year. Distillation began in November 1898 and apart from enforced closures during the two wars and the annual silent seasons, Aberfeldy has been in regular production for over a hundred years.

At various times in the company's long and successful history it has needed to buy additional distilleries to satisfy its requirements for whiskies suitable in its blend. The first was **Benrinnes** in 1922 and they took a twenty-one-year lease on **Royal Lochnagar** in the same year. The following year saw the purchase of **Ord**, **Pulteney**, Parkmore, **Oban** and **Aultmore** distilleries, and Port Ellen distillery on Islay was acquired in 1927. In 1915, Dewar's forged a 'close and permanent association' with James Buchanan & Co. Ltd and called the company Scotch Whisky Brands Ltd. In 1925, they merged with DCL.

In 1998, the company of John Dewar & Sons Ltd, its whisky stocks, bottling and blending facilities, Aberfeldy, **Aultmore** and two other distilleries not previously associated directly with Dewar's whisky were sold by the newly formed company, Diageo, to Bacardi.

A sketch of Aberfeldy distillery with the old maltings in the foreground that now house the 'Dewar's World of Whisky'.

During the year 2000 the new company invested in the development of the Dewar's World of Whisky. This is a 'unique exhibition and interactive centre' housed in the old maltings. This is the home of Dewar's White Label as well as Aberfeldy single malt and there is considerable emphasis in the exhibition to the importance in the methods used in blending.

Dewar's White Label

John Dewar established a wine and spirit business in Perth in 1846. In the late 1860s he began selling his blends in branded bottles rather than in small casks or plain stone jars. His son Tommy Dewar joined the company in 1881 and was a tremendous salesman establishing the Dewar's White Label blend in London during the 1880s and in many foreign markets during the 1890s. In 1892 he embarked on a two-year world tour and appointed thirty-two agents in twenty-six countries.

Dewar's White Label has been a successful brand for well over one hundred years. It is a big brand in the United States but sales have historically been very small in Britain. Worldwide sales are in the order of three million cases.

"You're a long time saying 'When,' Uncle."
"Why, of course it's Dewar's."

Above: *Towards the end of the nineteenth century and early twentieth century, Dewar's produced a range of high-quality promotional material in support of their sales effort behind their whiskies. A postcard, one of a series commissioned by Dewar's from Phil May the famous caricaturist, is dated 1902.*

1897 AULTMORE (Highland-Speyside)

Alexander Edward, whose whisky interests already included a partnership in **Craigellachie** distillery, built Aultmore in 1897 and a year later, shortly after buying **Oban** distillery, he put his two most recent acquisitions into a new company, Oban & Aultmore-Glenlivet Distilleries Ltd. Pattison's of Leith had an investment in the new company and, following their bankruptcy in December 1898, Aultmore's future was in doubt. The business struggled and after several setbacks during its first twenty years, Edwards sold Aultmore to John Dewar & Sons Ltd of Perth in 1923. Following the merger of Guinness and Grand Metropolitan in 1997, Aultmore was one of four distilleries sold as part of the deal to sell Dewar's White Label to Bacardi.

Aultmore, although fresh and smart in appearance, is functional, displaying little of its original late Victorian charm. The reconstruction of 1970 removed most traces of its Victorian origin. A quick glance at the distillery reveals that there is something amiss. There are no warehouses. They were demolished in 1996 and Aultmore's spirit is sent elsewhere for maturation. It is one of a number of distilleries that quietly produce a good malt whisky, ideal for blending, and as such its future can be assured.

1897 GLEN MORAY (Highland-Speyside)

In 1828, on a site close to the river Lossie to the west of Elgin, Henry Arnott built West Brewery. The site is near Gallow Hill, which until 1690 was the place of execution where murderers, thieves and witches were 'brint to the death, hanged by the craig, or droont'.

In 1897, Glen Moray Glenlivet Distillery Co. Ltd bought the brewery and converted it to a distillery. It is likely that the distillery began life owned by R.J. Thorne, the Greenock firm of whisky blenders that had owned **Aberlour** distillery since 1892.

Glen Moray suffered from the collapse of Pattison's in late 1898 and company distilling records show that they produced little whisky in 1902 and none at all in 1906, 1907, 1915 and 1918. The company went into liquidation and its present owners, then known as Macdonald & Muir, bought the distillery from the liquidators in 1921, three years after having bought **Glenmorangie** distillery.

Macdonald & Muir was a successful blending company and Glen Moray's malt whisky was ideal for their business. Apart from no production in 1932 and in two of the war years, Glen Moray has had a steady career. The floor maltings were replaced in 1958 by the Saladin box system that remained in operation until the late 1970s.

The malt whisky produced at Glen Moray is widely acclaimed by blenders and has been available as a bottled single malt since 1976. Interesting expressions of Glen Moray have been introduced in recent years where casks previously used in the wine trade to mature Chenin Blanc and Chardonnay are filled with mature whisky for an extra period of maturation, or *mellowing* as the owners describe it, thus creating an extra dimension of style.

1897 SPEYBURN (Highland-Speyside)

Charles Doig designed Speyburn distillery for Speyburn-Glenlivet Distillery Co. Ltd, a subsidiary of John Hopkins & Co. Ltd of London and Glasgow, blenders of Old Mull and Glengarry and owners since 1890 of **Tobermory** distillery. The distillery was built close to a good supply of water on a hillside site and because of its cramped location the production block was built three storeys high and the warehouses on two floors.

The owners were keen to produce their first casks of spirit before the end of 1897, the year of Queen Victoria's Diamond Jubilee. They achieved their objective, but only just. In the last week of December, with snow swirling around in the still house, with no glass in the windows or doors in their frames, just one butt bearing the date 1897 was produced.

John Hopkins used a quantity of the distillery's make for their own blends and acted as agents for the remainder. In 1916 DCL, eager to expand its export business, found the company's sales achievements overseas to be attractive and bought the company.

The distillery was closed during the Depression years of the early 1930s and between 1940 and 1947. During the war the distillery was used as base for two artillery units. In 1992 Speyburn was the second malt whisky distillery to be acquired by Inver House Distillers. It is a small distillery with one of the few remaining traditional raking systems installed in the mash tun and it has just two stills and two splendid wooden worm tubs to serve them. There is a treat in store for the industrial archeologist! Not only is the original Doig-designed pagoda roof still *in situ,* but the

old malting drums are still intact. Speyburn was the first distillery to install the Henning's pneumatic drum malting system and it continued in operation until 1968. There are six drums that were all driven by a twelve horsepower steam engine.

The distillery was built next to the Elgin to Craigellachie railway line but was not connected directly to it, preferring the use of horse and cart to take the whisky to nearby Rothes station and to fetch empty casks, barley and coal. This continued until the 1950s when tractor and trailer took over the role of the horse.

A final point about this splendid small distillery nestling in the Glen of Rothes is that because of its location close to the 'Hillock of the Gibbet' (the gallows where the criminals of Rothes were executed), locals know the distillery by its alternative name, Gibbet!

1897 TOMATIN (Highland-Speyside)

Built in 1897 by the Tomatin Spey District Distillery Co. Ltd, the distillery is to be found sixteen miles southeast of Inverness in one of the highest and most remote locations in Scotland. For the first sixty years of its life, the distillery was linked by means of a short branch line with the main railway connecting Inverness to the north and Perth to the south. Apart from a short silent spell between 1906 and 1908, the distillery was in steady production until the Second World War. Shortly after reopening in 1956, the number of stills increased from two to four, then by another two in 1958, a further four in 1961 and one extra in 1964, making a total of eleven. An extension to the still house in 1973 was equipped with twelve new stills, making a grand total of twenty-three! 1974 saw the distillery's greatest year of production with a colossal fourteen million litres.

Tomatin had the largest capacity to produce spirit of any malt whisky distillery in the country and it was highly automated to the extent that with a workforce of thirty, the distillery had a greater investment in equipment per worker than in an oil refinery. With such massive capacity came the problem of how best to utilise excess hot water and for a while Tomatin experimented with a commercial eel-farming project.

Speyburn distillery.

Although supplying most of the country's blenders with a malt distinguished by its peatiness and regarded by many as having the desirable properties of a Glenlivet, the company was badly affected by the very difficult trading conditions in the early 1980s and went into voluntary liquidation in 1985. In the following year the company was bought by a joint investment venture of two Japanese companies, Takara Shuzo & Co. Ltd and Okura & Co. Ltd, who had been long-standing customers of Tomatin.

The older half of the distillery is no longer in operation and the production in the newer half of just over two-and-a-half million litres of alcohol a year is similar to that of an average sized malt whisky distillery.

In 1997 the company bought J.W. Hardie and Co. Ltd and its Antiquary brand of blended whisky.

Tomatin distillery is a popular destination for visitors to the north of Scotland being conveniently situated just off the main A9 trunk road north of Aviemore.

1897 GLENDULLAN (Highland-Speyside)

The first Glendullan distillery was built close to the river Fiddich and by means of a large diameter water wheel generated sufficient waterpower to drive all the machinery. The distillery shared the railway sidings with neighbouring **Mortlach** distillery. The original owners were William Williams & Sons Ltd, whisky blenders of Aberdeen. After several mergers, Glendullan became part of DCL in 1926. The distillery's only period of closure was between 1940 and 1947 as the result of the restrictions on the supply of barley. The distillery was re-equipped in the early 1960s.

DCL, requiring additional malt whisky capacity to meet the growing export sales of the blended whiskies in the group, built an entirely new distillery on a site quarter of a mile upstream of the 'Old' Glendullan. Opened in 1972 this was a large distillery and its six stills are capable of producing four-and-a-half million litres of alcohol in a year. The two distilleries worked

in tandem until the decline in the industry in the 1980s when 'Old' Glendullan was added to the list of permanently closed distilleries.

1898 CAPERDONICH (Highland-Speyside)

Built in 1898 on the opposite side of the road from the original **Glen Grant** distillery, this, the last distillery to be built in Rothes, was given the distinguished name of Glen Grant No.2! Its purpose was to supply a whisky of similar quality to Glen Grant, but its product was not needed in the aftermath of the Pattison's crash and the distillery closed in 1902. With the strong upturn in the industry in the 1960s, the distillery was re-equipped, the original stills were retained and a second pair was installed. The distillery re-opened in 1967, this time with a brand new name, Caperdonich.

The whisky produced is quite different from Glen Grant and almost all of it is used for blending.

1898 GLENTAUCHERS (Highland-Speyside)

During the 1880s and 1890s, James Buchanan had been successfully developing sales of his Buchanan Blend in Britain, Germany, the United States, New Zealand and South America. He was adamant that his blend should be made up of mature malt and grain whiskies. His main supplier was W.P. Lowrie, the Glasgow firm of whisky brokers, blenders and bottlers, and it was in association with Lowrie that Buchanan built Glentauchers distillery midway between Rothes and Keith. It was laid out in the form of a square and a siding was built to link it with the nearby Aberdeen to Inverness railway line. The distillery was opened in June 1898 and the supply of water was so plentiful that a three-acre dam was built to supply a turbine that powered all the machinery. In 1905, Buchanan acquired Lowrie's business and it was in the same year that Buchanan Blend was renamed and registered as Black & White Whisky. The

Glentauchers in the 1970s whilst still part of DCL and licensed to James Buchanan & Co. Ltd.

company became part of DCL in 1925 and, apart from wartime closure, the distillery continued production until 1985 when, along with nine other DCL distilleries, it was closed. Its future looked bleak until 1989 when it was bought by Allied Distillers Ltd and re-opened.

1898 BENRIACH (Highland-Speyside)

John Duff, who had four years earlier built **Longmorn** distillery, constructed Benriach on a neighbouring site and when completed he merged the two distilleries into one company, Longmorn-Glenlivet Distilleries Co. Ltd. The company, through further acquisitions and takeovers, became part of Seagram of Canada in 1978. Benriach was closed after the Pattison's crash but the floor maltings were kept open to supply Longmorn. It was sixty-five years later, in 1965, when the whisky industry was experiencing great growth, that the distillery was refurbished and re-opened, and further enlarged in 1974. The maltings were occasionally used until their closure in 1999.

Benriach is available as a single malt, but the bulk of its product is used for blending.

1898 GLEN ELGIN (Highland-Speyside)

The construction of Glen Elgin distillery began in 1898. It was designed by Charles Doig for William Simpson, a former manager of **Glenfarclas** distillery and James Carle, a local agent for the North of Scotland Bank. Problems with financing the £13,000 project delayed completion until early 1900. Distilling began in May of that year but with the huge problems facing the whisky industry the distillery closed after only five months of production and was sold by auction in February 1901 for £4,000. The distillery was sold again in 1906 for £7,000 to J.J. Blanche & Co. Ltd, whisky distillers and blenders of Glasgow. On the death of J.J. Blanche in 1929, the distillery was again for sale and Scottish Malt Distillers bought it in the following year.

Until the 1950s Glen Elgin was almost entirely operated and lit by paraffin with additional power from a water turbine.

The distillery was largely rebuilt and enlarged in 1964 with a new mash house, tun room and still house with four new stills added to the original pair. It has been improved again in recent years and retains its worm tub system of condensing the spirit.

Glen Elgin was the last distillery to be built for sixty years. It had

a very haphazard start to life but its future was increasingly assured when its whisky became an essential malt in the White Horse blend.

1898 BENROMACH (Highland-Speyside)

Benromach distillery built on the outskirts of the Royal Burgh of Forres was another of Charles Doig's designs. Almost immediately after opening it was to suffer post-Pattison depression, followed by closure between 1931 and 1936 and ownership by the National Distillers of America from 1938 until 1953, when it became part of DCL. In 1968, DCL opened its large commercial maltings at Burghead, a few miles from Forres, and Benromach along with many other distilleries in the group, closed its floor maltings and obtained all of its malted barley from Burghead.

Benromach was one of eleven distilleries closed by DCL in 1983 and most of the distilling equipment was removed. In 1993 the Elgin-based whisky merchants, Gordon & MacPhail, bought the distillery and after re-equipping it with a Boby mill, a new mash tun, four rebuilt wash backs and two new stills, distilling commenced in October 1998.

The partnership of Messrs Gordon and MacPhail was established in 1895 in splendid new premises in the centre of the Royal Burgh of Elgin and they began to trade as 'Family Grocers, Tea, Wine and Spirit Merchants'. From those early days over a hundred years ago, the firm has grown from strength to strength as malt whisky experts. They have established themselves as the world's leading specialist supplier of bottled single malts. Their range of maturing malt whiskies is extensive and many rare and fascinating whiskies have been made available to whisky connoisseurs over the last fifty years. Gordon and MacPhail's range of single malt whiskies under the **Connoisseurs Choice**, 'Rare Old' and **Cask Strength** labels offers a whole spectrum of opportunities to sample Scotland's rarest drams, including a significant number from distilleries which have been closed for years.

1898 KNOCKANDO (Highland-Speyside)

In 1898 John Thompson, a spirit broker and Scotch whisky merchant from Elgin, bought a six-acre site close to the river Spey, adjacent to the Speyside railway line, and commissioned Charles Doig to build a distillery. Knockando was built of pinkish granite quarried from the nearby Elchies estate. The first mash was made

Above: *Benromach distillery.*

Below: *On a wall in Benromach's filling store, the DCL distillery team recorded the end of an era in 1983 when the last filling was made. When the distillery started production under its new owners in 1998 the new team of two recorded the happy event of the first filling!*

GORDON & MACPHAIL
FIRST FILLING 21ˢᵗ AUG 1998
R. MURRAY MANAGER
K. CRUICKSHANK PRODUCTION SUPERVISOR

LAST FILLING 24 MAR 1983
D. MACDONALD   MANAGER   WILLIE MCARTHUR
TOM. ANDERSON   BREWER   SANDY   CAMERON
B. GRIME   EXCISE   SANDY   MILNE
D. WATSON   R/ASST.   GEORGE INGRAM

LAST CASK No 1983 / 535

in May 1899 and already the future of this splendid new distillery was in serious jeopardy. With the chaos in the whisky industry that followed the crash of Pattison's, Thompson could find no one to buy his whisky. He stopped distilling in March 1900 and tried to sell the distillery. Three years later and for a consideration of £3,500, W. & A. Gilbey became Knockando's new owners and by October 1904 the distillery was producing whisky again.

In the period before the First World War, the distillery records show that a large amount of the spirit was filled into sherry, madeira and marsala butts. With the shortage of wood after the war, port pipes were also used to mature the spirit. A large part of the whisky made at Knockando was destined, along with the whiskies from Gilbey's other two distilleries on Speyside, **Strathmill** and **Glen Spey**, to be used in their successful blended whisky, Gilbey's Spey Royal. Knockando, through the various mergers and takeovers of the last thirty years firstly became part of the company owning J&B Rare blended whisky and then, more recently, was absorbed into the international drinks company, Diageo.

Knockando is readily available as a single malt and is only bottled when it is judged to be perfectly ready. The labels of the different bottlings of Knockando's 'vintage' single malt show the date of the

season of distillation and the year of bottling. In recent years the age of the 'vintage' has been between twelve and fifteen years.

J&B Rare

In 1831, when Alfred Brooks bought a prestigious London wine merchants established in 1749 by an Italian Giacomo Justerini, he renamed the company Justerini & Brooks. Their 'Club' blend of Scotch whisky was introduced in the 1880s and it found considerable favour with their customers, but it was to be J&B Rare, a blend specially produced for the American taste that was to be the toast not only of the town, but eventually the world. Introduced initially in the New York area immediately after the repeal of Prohibition in the United States and supported by huge promotional and advertising support, J&B Rare had become the leading brand of Scotch Whisky in the United States by the early 1960s. During the brand's period of rapid and sustained growth in the late 1960s, the company decided to build **Auchroisk** distillery on Speyside and ensure adequate supplies of a lightly flavoured malt to support further growth of sales in the brand. There are many countries around the world that appreciate a Scotch Whisky both light in style and light in colour. This is achieved by the careful selection of lighter styles of malt whiskies with little or no influence of Islay malts or whisky matured in sherry casks.

Above left: Knockando distillery in the 1920s.

Above right: Knockando single malt Scotch whisky.

Right: An example of J&B Rare's advertising in the UK in 1974.

Remote and austere. Dalwhinnie distillery in the early twentieth century when under American ownership.

J&B Rare was *the* successful blended whisky of the second half of the twentieth century and with annual sales in excess of six million cases it is the second largest brand of Scotch whisky in the world.

1898 DALWHINNIE (Highland-Speyside)

Traveling north to Inverness on the main A9 trunk road, it is something of a surprise to see set in the majestic but bleak landscape a very smart group of buildings which, at 1,073ft above sea level, is Scotland's highest distillery, Dalwhinnie. Although very remote, the small village of Dalwhinnie has long been an important meeting place. General George Wade used Dalwhinnie as a base when he was constructing a network of military roads in the wake of the first Jacobite uprising of 1715. The village was an important point on the north-south route used by cattle drovers when they were taking their animals to the markets of Crieff and Falkirk to the south. It was an ideal place to build a distillery with wonderful pure soft snow-melt water that collects in the Lochan an Doire-Uaine, 2,000ft high in the Drumochter Hills and then flows down to the distillery over rich peat along the Allt an t'Sluic burn.

In 1897, three local men invested £10,000 to build the Strathspey distillery on a site between the main Perth to Inverness road and the new Highland railway. A siding connected the distillery with the railway and production began in February 1898, but after only five months' production the distillery closed and the venture went into liquidation. New owners took over in November and renamed the distillery Dalwhinnie, but there was little hope of success in the prevailing conditions of gloom in the whisky industry. In 1905 the distillery was sold at auction for £1,250 to Cook & Bernheimer of New York and Baltimore. This was the first time in the history of Scotch whisky that a foreign company owned a distillery. Cook & Bernheimer had blending facilities in Leith and claimed that their blends would 'suit the American taste'. They no doubt did, but in 1919 with Prohibition in the United States, Dalwhinnie was sold to Macdonald Greenlees Ltd, distillers and blenders of Leith. Controlled by the prominent businessman Sir James Calder and already owning four other malt whisky distilleries including **Glendullan,** Macdonald Greenlees were the owners until 1926 when they were bought by DCL. The future of Dalwhinnie was assured when DCL licensed the distillery to James Buchanan & Co. Ltd, world famous for its Black & White and Buchanan blended whiskies.

A serious fire in 1934 closed the distillery for four years and it was again closed between 1940 and 1947. The distillery has on several occasions been refurbished, but it remains a small distillery with one pair of stills and traditional worm tubs. In 1989 the Dalwhinnie 15-year-old was selected to be one of two Speyside representatives in Diageo's range of Classic Malts. Smooth, sweet, honeyed, with hints of heather and peat, this is a malt with both delicacy and depth.

Distilling is not the only task of the employees of Dalwhinnie. The distillery is also Meteorological Office recording station No.0582, where daily data is gathered on many aspects of the weather, including in winter the depth of snow drifts, which can be as high as twenty feet.

Black & White

In the mid-1880s James Buchanan had established his own business in London selling a blended whisky in a distinctive black bottle with a white label. He called his blend The Buchanan Blend of Fine Old Scotch Whiskies and his customers often referred to it as Black & White. By the 1890s the brand was firmly established in London's clubs, hotels and music halls and he became the sole supplier of whisky to the House of Commons. The Black & White brand name was registered in 1905. Over the years many black and white subjects were used to advertise the brand, including the very popular black Scottish Terrier and white West Highland Terrier.

To ensure a good supply of the right malt whisky for his blend and in partnership with W.P. Lowrie he built **Glentauchers** distillery. Black & White enjoyed great export success and in 1915 to combat the growing competitive strength of DCL, Buchanan merged with John Dewar & Sons Ltd to form Scotch Whisky Brands. In 1925 they, along with John Walker & Sons Ltd, joined DCL.

The brand still sells well in various export markets and its clever and impactful advertising is remembered with much affection.

1899 ARDMORE (Highland)

By the mid-1890s the success of their blended whisky, Teacher's Highland Cream was such that William Teacher & Sons Ltd of Glasgow decided to build their own distillery and therefore guarantee a supply of quality malt whisky for the blend. To this day Ardmore is an important fingerprint malt in Teacher's Highland Cream. The site chosen was near ideal being adjacent to a main road and railway line in a rich agricultural area and with an abundant water supply from springs flowing down from Knockandy Hill. The name chosen for the distillery, Ardmore, was a little unusual in that it was named after a place near to the Teacher family home on the River Clyde, in the west of Scotland.

Buchanan's Black & White advertising in 1927.

COUNTRY LIFE, December 5, 1941

By Appointment to
HIS MAJESTY
KING GEORGE VI

A grand sight!

"Black & White" is always a grand sight to those who
appreciate a really well blended fine old Scotch Whisky.
The character of "Black & White" ensures that every drop
gives the utmost satisfaction.

"BLACK & WHITE"
It's the Scotch!

*Sir James Buchanan, who became Lord Woolavington in 1922, died in 1935.
An advertisement in* Country Life *in 1941 shows the brand simply known as
'Black & White'.*

The proximity to the railway was ideal for the despatch of whisky
to the company's blending and bottling facilities in King Street,
Glasgow, opened in 1898.

The distillery was doubled in size in 1958 and again in 1975. With
eight stills Ardmore is one of the largest in Scotland and until 2001
the stills were unusual in that they were all coal-fired, devouring
eighty-five tons of coal in a week. Steam coils now heat the stills.

Teacher's Highland Cream

In 1830 William Teacher entered the grocery and spirit trade and in
1834 he married the daughter of a Glaswegian grocer. With some
experience of blending whisky for sale in the family shop, he saw
the potential in selling whisky in specialised 'dram' shops. He
opened the first of these in the 1850s and built up a chain of
eighteen shops in Glasgow that survived for well over a hundred
years. They were unique to Teacher's. You could only buy
Teacher's whisky, Teacher's port, Teacher's brandy and beer. You
were not allowed to buy a round of drinks nor were you allowed
to smoke on the premises!

Teacher's Highland Cream was officially registered in 1884, six
years after the first consignment of the blend was sent to New
Zealand. To keep up with the increasing demand for the blend,
Teacher's built **Ardmore** in 1899 and bought **Glendronach**,
another Highland distillery, in 1960.

The Whisky of the Good Old Days

ESTABᴰ 1830

TEACHER'S
"HIGHLAND CREAM"
SELF-OPENING BOTTLE

Bury the Corkscrew!

*In 1913 Teacher's was the first company to produce a bottle closure
that did away with the need to open the bottle with a corkscrew.*

A Teacher's Dram shop in Glasgow.

The company produced the first self-opening bottle in 1913, thus doing away with the need to open whisky bottles with a corkscrew. William Teacher & Sons became a public company in 1949 and retained their independence until merging with Allied Breweries in 1976.

Teacher's Highland Cream has significant sales of around half a million cases in the UK and exports a million cases each year.

1960 TORMORE (Highland-Speyside)

After the Second World War, new life came back to a few distilleries that had been closed for more than just the war years. **Pulteney** in Wick and **Tamdhu** on Speyside are two examples of distilleries re-opened in 1947 after twenty or so years of closure. The first distillery to have been built from scratch and which was to survive the rest of the twentieth century was Tormore, built on Speyside and completed in 1960.

Two other distilleries had been built before Tormore in the post-war years but both were mothballed in the 1990s. William Delmé Evans, who subsequently was responsible for the building of the 'new' Isle of Jura distillery and then at a later date, **Glenallachie**, designed Tullibardine distillery in the Perthshire village of Blackford. Opening in 1949, Tullibardine was built on the site of an

old brewery and survived several changes of ownership until closed in 1995 by Whyte & Mackay.

In the small Speyside town of Keith, Seagram of Canada, already owners of **Strathisla**, one of Scotland's oldest distilleries converted the old Keith meal-mills into their second distillery and called it Glen Keith. In the second half of last century, Seagram acquired or built nine distilleries, all located on Speyside, and Glen Keith was mothballed in 1999 as a result of over-production in the group.

Designed by Sir Albert Richardson, President of the Royal Academy, and completed in 1960, Tormore distillery, set in landscaped gardens, is a very impressive solid structure with architectural details that combine style with some eccentricity. It was built for the American company, Schenley Industries Inc., owners of Long John whisky and in 1975, with the acquisition of Long John International, Tormore and **Laphroaig** distilleries became part of Whitbread, the English brewing company. In turn Allied Distillers Ltd became the owners of both distilleries when they bought Whitbread's spirit brands in 1990.

Some of this typical Speyside malt – sweet, medium-bodied with a hint of almonds – can be found as a bottled single malt, but most is used in the group's blends, notably Ballantine's.

1960 MACDUFF (Highland-Speyside)

Macduff was built in 1960 by a consortium of companies with interests in whisky blending. Classed along with **Inchgower** and the mothballed Glenglassaugh distilleries as a Coastal Speyside, the distillery is close to the river Deveron a few hundred yards from where it flows into the sea at Banff Bay.

The distillery was bought in 1972 by William Lawson Distillers Ltd, whisky merchants and blenders established in Dundee in 1849. Their William Lawson's blend has developed a successful market in Europe selling over a million cases each year. In 1980 the company became part of the General Beverage Corporation of Luxembourg and then a subsidiary of the Bacardi Corporation.

Macduff has five stills and they are a little unusual with their lyne arms leaving the swan's neck at a raised angle to produce more reflux and a lighter spirit. The condensers of the three spirit stills are also unusual in that they are fixed in a horizontal rather than the normal vertical position. Macduff is one of the few distilleries to blend on site and until quite recently had a small bottling facility in the distillery.

The official name of the single malt whisky from Macduff distillery is Glen Deveron.

1965 TOMINTOUL (Highland-Speyside)

With the ever-increasing demands for good quality malt whisky experienced in the early 1960s, two leading Glasgow whisky broker firms – Hay & Macleod and W. & S. Strong – formed Tomintoul Distillery Ltd and built a new distillery on Speyside which began production in July 1965. The company bought **Fettercairn** distillery in 1971 and through various takeovers and mergers the two distilleries became part of the American company, Fortune Brands. In 2000 Tomintoul was sold to the London-based independent blending firm, Angus Dundee.

1965 DEANSTON (Highland)

Deanston distillery is housed in a converted cotton mill, originally designed and built by Richard Arkwright in 1785. Most of the structural work dates from the 1830s and includes from that period a weaving shed with an impressive vaulted roof, a building ideal for its current use, maturing whisky.

James Finlay & Co. Ltd owned the mill and, given the buoyant conditions of the whisky industry in the 1960s, a leading blender, Brodie Hepburn, suggested conversion of the mill to a distillery. Finlay's agreed and backed the venture with two-thirds of the capital. Hepburn provided the rest of the capital and the management to run the business. The conversion of the main mill building to accommodate the large open mash tun, eight 60,000 litre stainless steel wash backs and four stills meant the removal of three very solid floors. The conversion took only nine months to complete and distilling began in October 1966.

The enthusiastic plans to use the whisky to support the development of a blended whisky did not materialise and Invergordon Distillers acquired the business in 1972. The distillery survived a further ten years before the recession in the industry closed the distillery in 1982. Mothballed for eight years, Deanston was bought by Burn Stewart Distillers in 1990 and re-opened the following year. Burn Stewart also own **Tobermory** distillery on the Island of Mull.

Most of the malt whisky produced at Deanston is used for blending. Burn Stewart supplies a number of supermarket groups

Right: *Two Speyside distilleries boast fine gardens. There is the **Glen Grant** Garden in Rothes and this excellent example in the Highlands in **Tormore's** extensive grounds.*

with their 'own label' brands and the company has been actively developing an export market with several blended whiskies including Scottish Leader.

Deanston is located very close to the river Teith and water for use in the distillery and as a source of power is drawn from the river a mile-and-a-half upstream and conducted to the distillery along a lade. The water is fed into two turbines at the phenomenal rate of ten million litres each hour and any power surplus to requirements in the distillery is fed into the National Power Grid!

Deanston's single malt used to be known as Deanston Mill but is now known simply as Deanston. The 12-year-old version is lightly peated, sweetish and with a noticeable malt flavour.

1966 LOCH LOMOND (Highland)

For three brief years in the early nineteenth century, close to the site of the present Loch Lomond distillery, there are records of a distillery of the same name having operated but like so many at the time it failed to survive.

Deanston's gleaming stills and spirit safe show well the care of the stillman.

The same fate could have been in store for the distillery established in 1966 in a collection of old industrial buildings alongside the river Leven, in what is now the Lomond Industrial estate in Alexandria, a small town near to Dumbarton to the north-west of Glasgow. The distillery closed in 1984 and it caught the eye of Alexander (Sandy) Bulloch, who was already a successful blender, bottler and wholesaler. To secure his company's continuing growth he bought the distillery, increased the capacity four fold and built several warehouses. To develop the company's ability to develop the business of blending whisky for the competitive retail and wholesale trade in the UK he built a grain whisky distillery in 1994 with annual production of over ten million litres of pure alcohol.

The malt whisky distillery is unique in having four stills of unusual design working alongside two recently installed traditional stills. The four stills have rectifiers installed in their cylindrical necks, capable of producing a range of styles of spirit, which when matured produce markedly different flavoured single malts. The two single malts of note are Loch Lomond and the 10-year-old Inchmurrin.

1968 GLENALLACHIE (Highland-Speyside)

Established in Edinburgh's port of Leith in 1815 as a firm of wine merchants, Charles Mackinlay & Co. Ltd soon became involved in the sale of malt whiskies and then developed their own range of blended whiskies. Mackinlay claims to have been the first blended whisky to be sold in a glass bottle, but this is disputed by Dewar's who believe they were first! Five successive generations ran the company until in 1961, in one of the fashionable moves by British brewing companies to invest in the Scotch whisky industry, Mackinlay's was acquired by Scottish & Newcastle Breweries Ltd. In need of a light and well-textured spirit for use in their two main blended whiskies, Mackinlay's Legacy and Finest Old Scotch Whisky, distillery designer William Delmé Evans was commissioned to build a new Speyside distillery to the west of Aberlour.

Completed in 1968, Glenallachie remained in S&N's hands until their whisky business was sold to Invergordon in 1985 and the distillery was immediately closed. In 1989, Pernod Ricard, owners of **Edradour** and **Aberlour** distilleries bought Glenallachie and immediately brought it back into production

Clan Campbell blended whisky is enjoying good sales growth in France, Spain and other European countries. In Britain it is known as House of Campbell and total worldwide sales exceed one million cases.

Glenallachie's architecture is clearly of the style of the 1960s.

Combining function with style, after almost thirty years Auchroisk remains a great credit to its designers.

1971 MANNOCHMORE (Highland-Speyside)

In 1971, with the ever-increasing demand for malt whisky to support the growing worldwide sales of blended whiskies, DCL built Mannochmore distillery on a site adjacent to **Glenlossie**. Both distilleries are licensed to John Haig & Co. Ltd and, although using the same supply of process water, Mannochmore, which does not have purifiers on the spirit stills, produces a slightly fuller flavoured spirit when compared with **Glenlossie**.

The period of over-production in the early 1980s meant the closure of Mannochmore between 1985 and 1989.

An interesting development in recent years was the introduction, for a limited period, of Loch Dhu 10-year-old Single Malt Scotch Whisky, also known as 'The Black Whisky'. Its unusual colour came from maturing Mannochmore spirit for ten years in casks that had been double charred before use.

1974 BRAEVAL (Highland-Speyside)

Built by Chivas Brothers in a remote hilly area nine miles south of Dufftown alongside Crombie water, a tributary of the river Livet, the Braes of Glenlivet distillery opened in May 1974. The distillery was planned at the outset to be a fully automated distillery operated on a 'one man per shift' basis. Initially equipped with three stills, two further stills were added in 1975 and a sixth in 1978. In 1994, to avoid any confusion in the name of the distillery with **The Glenlivet**, the Braes was renamed Braeval. In common with other distilleries in the group, the new spirit is sent by road tanker to Keith to be filled into casks and matured in the company's vast warehousing complex. Almost all of Braeval's entire make is used for blending. It is rarely seen as a bottled single malt.

1974 AUCHROISK (Highland-Speyside)

In the mid-1960s, International Distillers and Vintners, owners of the increasingly successful J&B Rare blended Scotch whisky, decided to support possible future sales growth by increasing production of the lighter styles of malt whiskies in the blend. Between 1968 and 1970, **Strathmill**, **Knockando** and **Glen Spey** distilleries were rebuilt or enlarged to double the level of their production. It soon became apparent to the company that even this extra capacity was insufficient for their future needs and they therefore planned to build an entirely new distillery. Their first and most fundamental task was to seek a site with water of the right quality and with an assured steady flow of the right quantity. Tests were carried out at Dorie's Well, on the side of a steep ravine at Mulben, located two miles from the river Spey on the Rothes to Keith road, and revealed a steady flow rate of nearly ten thousand litres an hour. This water was considered to be ideal for distilling, and after the water rights were secured for a reputed consideration of £5 million, Auchroisk distillery was built and the first spirit flowed in early 1974.

117

Fitted out with the best equipment of the day, Auchroisk has a six-roller Miag mill of German manufacture, a stainless steel semi-Lauter mash tun and eight stainless steel wash backs. The vast still house has four pairs of lantern-shaped stills all with near horizontal lyne arms destined to produce the required lighter spirit. Auchroisk is capable of making up to four million litres of spirit in a year and most of it is matured in ex-bourbon casks. A small amount intended for sale as the 'Singleton of Auchroisk' single malt whisky is, after spending ten years in cask, given between one and two extra years rounding off in dry oloroso sherry casks.

Great architectural skill was required to ensure that this large state-of-the-art distillery with its vast complex of warehouses capable of storing ten year's production did not become a 'blot on the landscape'. The architectural awards received by the distillery planners and architects are testimony to the success of all involved in one of the last great distillery developments in Scotland.

1975 ALLT A'BHAINE (Highland-Speyside)

Built in 1975 by Seagram at a cost of £2.7 million, Allt A'Bhaine, in its isolated location on the southern slopes of Ben Rinnes, was the ninth and last distillery to be built or acquired by Seagram in their first twenty-five years in Scotland. The distillery is of obvious contemporary design and is purposely functional with no warehousing and designed as **Braeval** to be operated on a 'one man per shift' basis.

1990 SPEYSIDE (Highland-Speyside)

Near the small Highland town of Kingussie and the ruins of General Wade's Ruthven Barracks there is a small group of five old mills that, when they were active, drew their power from the river Tromie, a tributary of the Spey. For seventeen long years between 1960 and 1977, one man, a drystane dyker by the name of Alex Fairlie, restored these five mills, which over the years had been used for threshing, carding, sawing timber and milling meal and flour. In 1990 the owner, George P. Christie, who had an extensive career in the whisky industry decided to equip the largest of the mills as a distillery. Using new equipment from local suppliers, including a stainless steel Glen Spey semi-Lauter mash tun and two new stills fabricated by Forsyth of Rothes, the first spirit was produced in December of that year.

The distillery takes its name from the large distillery that was built in Kingussie in 1895 and survived only until 1911.

All that is needed in a distillery is under the roof of one mill at Speyside distillery.

Most of the make from Speyside is sent to Glasgow and is used for blending, but a small amount has been used as Drumguish, a single malt of no stated age which takes its name from the local area. With the availability of aged stocks of the first year's production a Speyside 8-year-old has been released and a 10-year-old version has recently been made available.

1990 KININVIE (Highland-Speyside)

Kininvie distillery was built on a site very close to **Balvenie** distillery and its main purpose in life is to distil in its four stills the wash that has been prepared on its behalf in the mash tun and wash backs of **Balvenie**. The whisky produced at Kininvie is all used for blending.

1995 ISLE OF ARRAN (Island)

It is a fitting conclusion to our journey through time to see embodied in the last of the distilleries to be built in the twentieth century, a few of the vital factors that are the route to success and survival in this unique industry. When the Isle of Arran distillery was on the drawing board there was, and still is, no need for new distilling capacity let alone a new albeit small distillery. In June 1995, when the distillery was producing its first spirit, Whyte &